making
MUSIC

cooperatively

Using Cooperative Learning in Your
Active Music-Making Classroom

making

MUSIC

cooperatively

Using Cooperative Learning in Your
Active Music-Making Classroom

Carol Huffman

GIA Publications
Chicago

— To my son, Nathan —

Making Music Cooperatively
Carol Huffman

GIA Publications, Inc.
7404 S. Mason Ave.
Chicago, IL 60638
www.giamusic.com

G-8126

ISBN: 978-1-57999-864-6

Cover Design and Layout by Martha Chlipala

CONTENTS

CONTENTS

Acknowledgments

This book would not have been possible without the cooperative learning workshops and courses I have taken over many years that helped me develop creative ways of teaching children. Bill Tenney's cooperative learning workshop, the Fresno Pacific College cooperative learning course taught by Douglas Bartsch, and the Ashland University cooperative learning course featuring *A Guidebook for Cooperative Learning* by Dee Dishon and Pat Wilson O'Leary helped contribute to the cooperative learning ideas in my Orff Schulwerk classroom. In addition, I must thank all Lt. Col. John Glenn Elementary teachers and students who provided me with feedback and support for twenty-six years. Thanks also to the many teachers throughout the United States who encouraged me at the many workshops I gave and inspired me to write this book on cooperative learning.

I thank my colleague and friend Dr. Robert de Frece of the University of Alberta in Edmonton, Canada for his excellent advice and editorial assistance. Also, thanks to Andrew Kuster, whose copyediting helped make my writing shine. Thanks to Jenna Kirk, my former student teacher and now a terrific teacher in her own right, for her help in editing. She makes me so proud of her teaching. Steph Griffin, another former student teacher; Jean Dayton, neighbor, friend, and fellow book-lover; Joanna Quandt, friend and psychologist advisor; Memory Blodgett, my most loving friend, who encouraged me all the way; and my beloved husband, Phil, all helped contribute to make this book a reality.

INTRODUCTION

SHARE WITH ME A DREAM

Imagine entering a classroom full of excitement. A classroom that buzzes with activity and enthusiasm. A classroom full of joyful social interaction, a desire to excel, and where students are happy, motivated, and brimming with ideas.

Imagine being the teacher in that classroom, walking from group to group, observing as learning takes place among the students—without directly being involved in the teaching.

For many teachers, this might sound like an impossible dream, but I'm thrilled to tell you it is not. I've seen it happen many times through an approach called cooperative learning.

When cooperative learning is set in place, the students become teachers of other students, and the teacher becomes the facilitator. Ideas come from the students, and develop into learning and activity. Students become more independent and responsible for their own learning, and are more capable of applying what they have learned to solve problems within the framework of the subject.

The teacher clearly will realize that the students are excited to learn, to share their ideas, and to work with their peers. And the teacher learns, too! Cooperative learning creates a happy, enthusiastic environment that benefits everyone, and helps students thrive in the 21st Century.

My dream for you is that you discover how cooperative learning can enhance and even transform your music teaching, and provide your students with opportunities to embrace music with the joy and natural abandon that children possess.

How I Got Started

It was only by chance that I discovered cooperative learning as a form of teaching. I had, of course, used groups in my teaching, but I felt there was something missing. I was looking for a way to create group work that produced better quality results.

During coursework for my Master's degree at Baldwin-Wallace College in Ohio, I took a class called Cooperative Learning. Almost immediately, I was hooked, and took many other related courses. I began to utilize the strategies I had learned from my coursework in my own elementary classrooms with my first through sixth grade students. They were to become my experimental "guinea pigs." Little did I know then, but I was soon to embark upon some of my most rewarding teaching experiences of all. Those wonderful children provided me with such an enthusiastic response that I have used the cooperative learning approach in my teaching and workshops ever since. Cooperative learning literally changed my teaching (and my learning) forever.

This book is intended as a guide to help educators incorporate the principles of cooperative learning in their classrooms in a practical, hands-on way. Over the years, I have developed successful approaches for group learning that have continuously grown, and never were static. One of the most rewarding results of cooperative learning is seeing new ideas evolve and grow into even more ideas. Most rewarding of all is seeing the dynamics of children as they learn to work and make music together. In my experience, no other book, theory, or teaching method can begin to approach the sheer joy that erupts in the cooperative learning environment.

Do you dream about an enriched, exciting classroom? With cooperative learning, you can make the dream come true.

CHAPTER ONE

PREPARING FOR SUCCESS

One of the delights of cooperative learning is seeing your students become more musical, more knowledgeable, and more excited about their lessons. However, before that can happen, you as the teacher must understand how to create a cooperative learning environment, how to organize your classroom, and how to utilize strategies to promote group interaction and creativity.

Most teachers use groups in their classrooms, but this common approach to learning does not always produce good results. Elementary-age children do not inherently have the necessary cooperation, communication, skill sets, or comprehension to perform productively by themselves in groups. In my early teaching experiences, I myself mistakenly assumed that students automatically knew how to work in groups. I also made the mistake of assuming that each child possessed basic skills: the ability of each student to remember his or her assigned group, for example. I also mistakenly assumed that each student would be willing to spontaneously share his or her work within the group. This book will help you avoid some of my early mistakes and help prepare you for success.

As the teacher, you will need to create goals for your students, provide clear instructions, develop guidelines for group interaction, and monitor activities—all on top of teaching the lesson for the day. At first this can seem overwhelming, but you will discover, as I did, that students quickly see the benefits of working together. They are eager to begin working as soon as they enter the classroom, they develop group loyalty, and their enthusiasm for learning increases significantly. When each student is given an opportunity to contribute in the classroom, they never forget the feeling of accomplishment this brings. When all students expect to contribute individually during every lesson and know their contribution will be respected and valued, their delight in returning to the classroom will remain high. Even shy students will ultimately come to feel this pleasure if they feel unthreatened. But certainly, the teacher needs to reinforce all of this by teaching the students to cooperate.

Cooperative learning is a technique that uses groups or teams to problem-solve tasks to learn. It demands that the team spend adequate time together to develop a sense of community within the team. When this community atmosphere is achieved, each team member begins to experience a real feeling of shared responsibility. In order for this to occur, time spent together learning about each other is imperative. Following this achievement of communal sense, genuinely joyful music learning can be accomplished.

Ensure that the groups you assemble to learn together are truly cooperative. As Johnson and Johnson recommend: "Cooperative learning groups are characterized by positive interdependence, individual accountability, face-to-face promotive interaction, the appropriate use of interpersonal and small-group skills, and group processing. It is cooperative learning groups that promote higher achievement, more positive relationships among students, and greater psychological health."[1]

In my teaching, I was fortunate to have a supportive staff that enabled me to develop my cooperative learning classroom with relatively few obstacles. But besides the nurturing support of staff and colleagues, a teacher may need to address other issues in a cooperative learning classroom. Once, a worried parent called me about the group in which I had placed her child. The parent was concerned about bullying. I tried to explain that cooperative learning was a teaching technique to help deal with problems such as bullying, and that her child would benefit from remaining in the particular group in which I had placed her. But the parent adamantly refused to see my point of view, and so I had to remove the student from the group and place her in another. In this situation, the bias of the parent had a direct impact on the child's learning experience. And, though the child still had a successful experience, I feel that her learning would have been deeper if she had remained in the original group. Cooperative learning can have a very positive impact on children who come from a biased home environment, because students discover that in cooperative grouping there are fewer differences between students and more similarities than they might have expected. I encourage you to give some thought about how to overcome the concerns that parents or staff may have about your cooperative learning approach. I recommend that before you begin using cooperative learning, you send a brief letter home explaining what cooperative learning is and how their student will benefit.

At first, you may need to overcome the negative opinions and (seldom repressed) comments of other staff and teachers. Since

---

1   D. W. Johnson and R. T. Johnson, "The role of cooperative learning in assessing and communicating student learning" *1996 ASCD Yearbook: Communicating Student Learning*, edited by T. R. Gusky (Alexandria, VA: Association for Supervision and Curriculum Development, 1996).

most teachers utilize groups, they may have their own bias about how effective cooperative learning can be—and especially how it can be applied to a music classroom without chaos. So prepare to be challenged at times. When someone questions you, it's your opportunity to explain cooperative learning and its tremendous benefits for both students and teachers. Use the opportunity to share with any cynics your excitement in seeing your groups work together to achieve successfully not only the day's lesson, but in seeing them build their long-term confidence and enthusiasm. When you begin, you may have some skeptics, but eventually your results will speak for themselves.

Nearby classrooms will tolerate your "chaos" when you invite the skeptical teacher into your class to hear the creative results at the end of the lesson. Teachers are more likely to support cooperative learning when they see firsthand the creative way that students solve problems and get results. Visiting teachers also will notice that students are eager to come to music class and that the principal will need to manage fewer disruptive students. My experiences have produced amazing results with students who are severely emotionally disturbed. These students become excited to attend music class, and their social skills greatly improve after participating in cooperative learning teams. Finally, I have observed that students achieve better skills when they are involved in teaching each other. The inherent healthy competition within the team and between the teams gives impetus to get better and better at the musical skill being taught. This, too, will gradually become apparent the longer you use cooperative learning.

Throughout this book, I use the term "active music making," which will be familiar to teachers using Orff-Schulwerk, Kodály, Dalcroze, and Gordon approaches. A great resource concerning these teaching approaches is the Alliance for Active Music Making website at www.allianceamm.org. This website has valuable information that can point you in the right direction for any approach to active music making. And anyone using an active music making approach other than these four will still be able to adapt cooperative learning to his or her situation or expertise. I encourage you to think continually of new ways to incorporate cooperative learning structures in your daily lessons. Without a doubt, you will not regret the time you invest to plug cooperative learning into your own active music making classroom.

CHAPTER TWO

TAKING TIME TO SETTLE IN

What is cooperative learning? "*Cooperative learning is a successful teaching strategy in which small teams, each with students of different levels of ability, use a variety of learning activities to improve their understanding of a subject.* Each member of a team is responsible not only for learning what is taught but also for helping teammates learn, thus creating an atmosphere of achievement. Students work through the assignment until all group members successfully understand and complete it."[2]

Before using cooperative learning, it is important to share the goals with your students. Discuss how cooperative learning will benefit them. My reasons for using cooperative learning begin with the fact that we live in a global economy. It is rare today that a person works alone, even if he or she works at home. Most often, people work together to get results. Our nation—and our world—is such a wonderful mixture of ethnicity and religions, and a deeper understanding of different ethnicities and religions enables us to get along better despite our differences. When social skills are honed to

2 David Johnson and Roger Johnson, *Cooperative Learning*, http://www.clcrc.com/
   pages/cl.html (October 2001).

make people kinder and more tolerant of differences, the results of our work improve. It makes sense for a teacher to introduce students to the real world within the classroom. Certainly, we teach our specific subject matter, but why not also teach skills that will help the students deal with the real world that they will become a part of through their work and life's contributions?

It seems that, as adults, many of us are not as successful as we could be dealing with our own anger management, physical and verbal abuse, relationship connections, and co-existing with others in civil ways. In order for our students to become more skillful in these areas, they need to practice their social skills again and again. Using cooperative learning techniques while students study concepts in music class allows them to practice healthy social skills that they will use in their future lives. By mixing students into heterogeneous teams, we give each student the experience of working with other students who are different from them. A teacher should explain this before beginning the actual experience. Discussing these ideas with the whole class prepares the students for the cooperative learning experience before it actually begins. It also alleviates potential problems that might result due to differences within each team. When students are prepared to try learning and working with different kinds of students for good reasons, they are more likely to try new things.

I begin my student's cooperative learning classroom experience with a demonstration. To the entire class, I pass out pictures that are almost (if not exactly) the same. I pass out colored swatches of fabric that are exactly the same. I ask the students to note things about these items. The students find that almost every response is the same as what another student would have said. Have each student describe the picture and the color swatch to see how many different observations are said about these same things.

Now, I repeat the activity with pictures and fabric swatches that are each entirely different from one another. Using these new sets, the students' observations will be entirely different from the pictures and fabric swatches of the first observation round. Record how many different responses you get. What did the students find out about things that are the same (or almost the same) and things that are different? Explain to them that when they get into their cooperative learning teams, there will be some teammates who are similar to them and others who will be vastly different, just as with the images and fabric swatches. They may experience more ideas and participate in situations that they really never considered before because of their differences. And their experiences will be richer for these differences.

Practicing Cooperative Learning Skills

Conflict Resolution

A great way to start practicing cooperative learning skills is by teaching conflict resolution. On a piece of paper or a chalkboard, list the following tools that students can use to resolve any conflict:

- Compromise
- Voting
- Rock, paper, scissors game
- Flipping a coin
- Another idea

Then, write two rhythms that begin the same way but end in two different ways. The two rhythms should present the students with conflicting results for which they as a team need to determine one solution. Ask each team to decide on their one preferred resolution for the rhythm. In making this decision, each team can use any of your listed conflict resolution tools for its resolution.

When it is time to share the rhythms that each team chose, ask how each team resolved their conflict. Have them explain to the class the method they used to resolve their conflict and whether everyone was happy with the resolution.

Students can practice these kinds of activities over and over with different musical concepts and experiences. Finding resolutions to conflicts in a game situation teaches skills that gradually will make arguing in class a thing of the past. The students like to be able to solve problems in a quick and easy manner.

KINDNESS

Students find role-playing to be both fun and informative—and a good way for a teacher to demonstrate kindness. For example, whenever a student says something rude to another student, I always echo the rude remark in class. I usually exaggerate the way the student inflected their rude remark so they know my imitation was done in jest. When the students hear their teacher mimicking them being unkind, they laugh and realize what they sound like when they are rude. They learn that they must then speak more kindly to the other students. But, it is important for a teacher to be careful with this strategy, so that the students know that you are not criticizing anyone, but rather correcting their behavior.

To practice kind interaction, distribute scenarios to each team and ask them first to perform each scenario using unkind remarks, and then to repeat the same scenario using kinder remarks. For example, have the teams create a sound piece depicting a rainstorm. The piece must have a beginning, middle, and an end section. How will each student practice kindness in deciding which instruments the team will use? How long will each section of the piece be? How will the team decide, using kind words, which student will play which instrument? When each team shares its piece for the class, they also should share the kind words that the team used to get the task accomplished.

Body Language

It is important that students become aware of how body language can impact others. To demonstrate for the class, I begin with my body in a posture that shows distaste without using words. Then, I grow into angry body language without using words, and then I change so that ultimately my body language shows happiness. I ask the class to discuss with a partner nearby how they knew how I felt without using any words.

For my next demonstration, I distribute pictures depicting emotions to each team. I ask them to display the emotion in the pictures without using words. First, within each team, each team member should have a chance to depict the emotion of the picture given to the team, without words. Then, each team should take a turn all at once in front of the other teams. Have the other teams decide what emotion each team was showing with its body language.

A particularly important time to teach body language skills is when a teacher first assigns students to their new teams. Before we assign new teams, we practice showing emotions with our faces to show disappointment, anger, happiness, and neutrality. Using our faces to show how we feel can make each student feel accepted or rejected when they discover who else is in their new teams. We don't even need to use words to show these feelings. Then, we discuss which face shows the best way not to hurt anyone else's feelings during this emotional time. The students usually decide that neutrality is the best way not to offend anyone. In this way, no one else is aware whether a person is disappointed or happy when they learn who else is in their new team. The students thus learn that it is all right to have feelings about each other, but that during this important time they should keep their feelings inside so as not to hurt the feelings of other people on their team.

GETTING SETTLED INTO A NEW TEAM

The first day of team assignments is exciting—it can be either joyful or disappointing for the new teammates. Before and during the time I assign the students to teams, I remind them of their body language, kindness, sharing, conflict resolution skills, appropriate listening behaviors, responsibility to work equally, the richness of their differences, the need for politeness, and their knowledge of how to get the job done. These are all things we have talked about, experienced, and practiced before I first assigned teams. Once the students are in their new teams, it is time to get to know each other before we try musical tasks together.

It's important to begin each lesson with a team-building activity. These activities take only a few minutes, but they enrich the teammates' loyalty to each other, and as a result the students end up producing better quality work on their assigned tasks. Creating a team name gives each team a sense of importance, identity, and personality. This also gives the teacher a chance to see how teams begin to work together. It is always immediately interesting to observe the team dynamics. Within each team, a teacher quickly can see:

- Who is the leader?
- Who is laid back?
- Who is the arguer?
- Does the team make decisions quickly enough to accomplish a task?
- Does the team remember to share, and do they all work equally?

If problems occur, the teacher is responsible to observe and make comments to the teams; a gentle reminder goes a long way. This may involve showing the team experiencing a problem a poster with helpful hints for successful cooperative learning—pointing out one key behavior or strategy might be all a teacher needs to do to help a struggling team.

On the first day, it often helps to carry out most of your lesson by modeling and teaching general concepts. Requiring teams to accomplish too much without prior cooperative learning experience might be too much to ask at first, especially with younger students.

Part of what makes future collaboration successful is to discuss what helped in each collaborative effort and what did not. Continuous self-evaluation is critical for students to learn social skills and build team interdependence. At the end of the first assigned task, ask the class to think about what worked best to allow them to collaborate or accomplish the task, and then let them share their observations. Ask the class to discuss what didn't work and caused the task either not to be accomplished or not be of high quality, and once again let them share their observations.

COOPERATIVE LEARNING DISCIPLINE

APPROPRIATE VOICES

At first, a cooperative learning classroom might seem chaotic. You might think that you cannot cope with all of the excitement, noise, and activity. The times before and between tasks can be especially chaotic unless you have a plan. Before the teams begin to talk and get off track, establish a quiet sign so that you won't need to shout over their voices. The quiet sign can be a non-verbal cue that you can use to indicate to everyone that it is time to devote their attention to you. I use the "1, 2, 3, 4, 5" sign. I raise my hand and silently count out my fingers:

- One, the students need to look at the teacher.
- Two, their mouths need to close.
- Three, they need to begin to listen.
- Four, sit still.
- Five, they need to focus on what will be said the next moment.

This "1, 2, 3, 4, 5" sign gives all the students time to get ready to take instructions. A student sees the teacher begin the finger count with a raised hand and will remind his or her teammates also to join in the count. Soon the class is silent and ready for instructions.

In class, students need to practice speaking with the appropriate voice register and dynamic level. I refer to these as *outdoor* voices, *indoor* voices, and *six-inch* voices. A six-inch voice is at a dynamic level appropriate for a person to speak with someone else literally six inches apart, face to face. I point out to the students that they would not want to use an outdoor voice or even an *across the room* voice when they are that close to another person—it would hurt their ears. A six-inch voice is appropriate for teamwork. We practice each of the voices and use our "1, 2, 3, 4, 5" quiet sign in between to make sure that students practice that, too.

When enthusiasm builds or arguments erupt, the register and dynamic level of voices often get out of control. For these instances, I display *yellow*, *red*, and *green* signs. The *yellow* sign means that the classroom is getting a little too loud, and they need to remind themselves to use their six-inch voices. Further, when the yellow sign makes its appearance, it is a warning that the team's turn to work together will end and what they have accomplished to this point, even if they are not finished, will be their end result if they do not bring their voices or instruments down to a six-inch volume level. If the *red* sign appears (usually after a yellow sign), the students know that their working period is ended, and that they did not reach the appropriate six-inch voice level. They must discontinue their work. What they have accomplished is all that will be assessed. A *green* sign (usually after a yellow sign) means they are on their way again to working together in an appropriate dynamic environment. It is important to practice with these signs so the students understand that you say what you mean and mean what you say. Being consistent with the classroom noise level is imperative. Students soon learn to keep their voices and instrument sounds to a level where all can work comfortably. A comfortable environment helps the students better be prepared with their tasks.

These descriptions of dynamics pertain not only to voices, but also to playing instruments. Because some instruments can be extremely loud, practicing with instruments using six-inch dynamics is very important in an active music-making classroom. If the students need to play *fortissimo* for a task, I ask them, during practice time, to use their body energy using large motions to show their dynamic, but

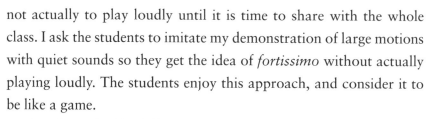

not actually to play loudly until it is time to share with the whole class. I ask the students to imitate my demonstration of large motions with quiet sounds so they get the idea of *fortissimo* without actually playing loudly. The students enjoy this approach, and consider it to be like a game.

Another valuable skill to help limit the noise level in the classroom is for students to speak only one at a time. Taking turns to speak also teaches students an important social skill. Listening to others without interrupting is difficult for some children, especially those who are enthusiastic, gregarious, and eager to be creative. Respecting the opinions and suggestions of others is a skill that takes time to develop.

Two good ways to teach students to speak one at a time are using a *talking stick* and using *plastic chips*. A talking stick is just that: when a person holds the talking stick, the others are to listen quietly. The stick is passed around so that each teammate has a turn to speak. Or, sometimes I pass out five *plastic chips* to each team member. When a student wishes to speak, he or she places a chip in the center of the team's circle. Then the others must listen to what he or she has to say. The students can use their chips in any order, but when a student's chips are used up, that student cannot talk until the team discussion is complete. The teacher must explain these tasks clearly, and can use role modeling to make tasks easy for students to understand. Then, students can teach each other. For example, have one team demonstrate to all the others the social skill you want to teach—like using the talking stick. The teacher might be part of the demonstration, playing the role of the interrupter so that students can observe what inappropriate behavior looks and sounds like. Students often giggle at the teacher's role during these demonstrations, but they always remember the lessons learned through them.

ASKING QUESTIONS

Despite clear instructions from the teacher, sometimes students will have questions during tasks, and students need to learn the least disruptive way to find answers. I tell the students that, when a question arises in a team, the first thing they should do is ask their teammates for an answer. If no one in the team knows the answer, one person chosen by the team will turn to a nearby team and ask them if they know the answer. If that fails, their representative may ask another nearby team. If the question has still not been answered, the time has arrived for all of the team members to raise their hands to call the teacher for an answer. When the students use this approach to answering questions, the classroom is quieter and the students act as their own teachers.

When students become their own teachers, they retain more knowledge. This allows the teacher to focus on the class as a whole, and manage student behaviors without interrupting the flow of the group learning process or being distracted answering questions for one team after another when it's easier for them to get the answers from each other. The teacher can constantly circulate throughout the room and observe the progress of each team with the assigned task. If a teacher spends time answering questions, it interrupts observing students. In turn, students begin to notice the lack of attention given to their behavior, which results in potential disruption of the cooperative learning environment. A teacher must always be aware of what is going on in the room when he or she assists teams. My students always say that I have eyes in the back of my head—an important skill to acquire.

TIME MONITORING

Depending on the activity, a teacher might decide to keep track of time him or herself, or a teacher might assign one member of each team to be the timer. The timer's role is to monitor the time for each step of a task, determined in advance by the teacher. However, when a teacher keeps track of time him or herself, there is more flexibility to say to the teams, "You have ten more minutes," when the teams clearly need more time. Or to say, "You have two more minutes for this part of the task, and then you must move on." When I am timer, I can determine if the teams are completing the task more quickly or more slowly than I had anticipated. I can give teams more or less time, depending on the circumstances. (If one team continually gets their task accomplished much more quickly than the others, I find it helpful to have another short activity or "bonus activity" prepared for that team so that they don't lose focus on the task.)

Sometimes having a "timer" in the team might lead to greater autonomy of the team if the teacher knows the students can handle this role. To make each student in a team feel more valued, it can be useful to give everyone a special role such as:

- "Choir/Orchestra Director"—in charge of performance technique
- "Efficiency Expert"—much like the "timer" but also helps to make things run more smoothly
- "Idea Expert"—in charge of making sure a team's results are creative
- "Dynamics Expert"—in charge of volumes in the music
- "Articulation Expert"—in charge of making musical creations by suggesting accents, legato/staccato, etc.
- "Peacekeeper"—in charge of resolving any conflicts within the team
- Etc...

You can make jobs for whatever task you are working on (composing, singing, choreography, anything). When everyone has a specific role, each student approaches the activity with something particular in mind for the end result's collaborative success.

For success in your active music-making cooperative learning classroom, time well-spent on non-musical preparations adds up to more time to make music in the end. But a teacher needs to start from scratch. Assume that students know nothing about getting along together, know nothing about using their time wisely, about how to find out unknown information independently, or know how to work quietly. Even if they do, they need to learn how to improve on these skills for your classroom. For these important issues, students must practice, discuss, and practice again. The more practice the students have with these basic cooperative skills, the better they will be able to create music together.

CHAPTER THREE

GETTING STARTED

Organization is the key to success in cooperative learning. When both your bookkeeping and your classroom are in order, your students will know how to organize themselves and will independently retrieve and put away materials and equipment without messing up the order of the classroom.

To organize your bookkeeping, I recommend that you create class lists for each classroom with columns displaying number and letter groupings. (See example on the next page.)

Assign each student a team letter and a number within the team. I usually assign four students per team. But, depending on the size of the class and whether the number of students is even, there might be three or five in a team. However, I find that four is the optimum number for working together cooperatively. Too many students in a team make decision-making difficult. And with less than four, the ideas can sometimes be skimpy. At the beginning of each grading period, I assign new teams. Our grading period lasts nine weeks. The students remain in the same teams throughout the entire nine weeks. This amount of time together gives them an opportunity to really

Names of students, their team letters, and number within their team.

Name	Team Letter	Number within Team
Joe	A	1
Sarah	A	2
Jessie	A	3
Pete	A	4
Clare	B	1
Tom	B	2
Susie	B	3
Matt	B	4

get to know each other, to feel comfortable working together, and to develop team loyalty. And good camaraderie during their work on creative tasks produces better results.

Very often, my students sit on the floor to work, so I scatter signs with the team letters on them on the floor. When I first assign the students to teams, I instruct them to sit in a circle around their letter, for example:

I also assign each student a number within each team. I number either in alphabetical order or arbitrarily so that no one feels slighted. (Incidentally, I have found that first graders *all* want to be number one, so I assign them colors rather than numbers: blue, red, yellow, and green. That way, no particular person is "number one.")

After the students get their team letter and number, we play a game. I call out numbers, and whenever a student hears their number, they stand up. At first I call out numbers slowly, but soon I speak the numbers more rapidly. Then I sometimes call out two or three numbers at a time! The classroom starts to look like a jack-in-the-box—They love popping up and down. It's fun, but at the same time they are learning an important skill that they will use for their entire time together.

Games help the students remember their team letter. Sometimes I ask each team to create a team name beginning with the letter of their assigned team. ("Adventurers" for team A, "Boomerangs" for team B, "Crazies" for team C, and so on.) To point younger children in the right direction, I ask them to think of a candy, animal, color, or fruit that begins with the team letter.

Many activities require a teacher to make fair choices about who goes first or whose turn it is next. For my students to feel confident that my spontaneous choices are fair, I use spinners. I purchased some small, undecorated cardboard spinners from an educational store. On one spinner, I wrote the letters for the teams, and on another spinner are the numbers for the individuals within each team. (For younger students, I use a spinner that I colored for the individuals in each team.) When we need to choose which team should do something,

I spin the letter spinner. When we need to choose which individual should do something, I spin the number or color spinner. I might say, "All the blues get a non-pitched instrument," or "All the number twos and fours sing my solfeggio." Spinners simplify and speed up the way I call on students. Since my lessons last only thirty five minutes, this efficiency gives me more time to teach. You can buy spinners online from Sharp School Services (www.sharpschoolservices.com/ blank_spinners or call 1-800-578-9972). But many teacher's supply retailers sell blank spinners so you can create your own.

Spending time on team-building activities like naming and numbering is crucial at this early stage. Not only does it help the students remember which team they belong to, it also gives me an immediate indication of the team dynamics. I observe who the leaders are and who does not contribute as often in the decision-making process. I also can see how quickly each team solves tasks. All of this helps me better be able to redirect and review their cooperative learning skills.

It's also critical that the teams learn from and acknowledge each other's achievements. After each task, each team should share its solution with the whole class. And the other teams should show appreciation of their creations through applause, since acknowledgment of everyone's creative effort is important. Any sincere creation is worthy of appreciation—some more than others— and this will become more apparent as your journey with cooperative learning continues.

When the next music class comes around, the students usually remember what they learned in the first class. All I must do for them to remember their team letter is to remind them of the team name or the animal they thought of last time. Nevertheless, sometimes upon entering the music classroom after forming a new team, students give me panicked stares when they see the team letters on the floor. If students forget, I make sure that their teammates who remember help those who forgot by reminding them they are in their team. I also review which number within each team everyone is. Then, after everyone knows their team and number, I have the children perform a team-building activity (see chapter 4).

Organizing the Classroom

With cooperative learning, organizing your materials and equipment is vital, especially when different classes use the same materials and equipment. Creating a place for everything and labeling everything is necessary to keep things accessible for each different lesson. Each of my shelves is labeled with a place for each instrument, and each instrument has an identical corresponding label.

I group all the pitched instruments together in one place and all non-pitched instruments together in another. I keep my non-pitched instruments on a table and, on a piece of colorful paper, I have outlined the shape of each instrument and labeled it. My table has the non-pitched metals at the right (corresponding to their higher level of sound, parallel to a piano keyboard), the non-pitched woods in the center, and the skins (sounding lowest) on the left. Each instrument location has an outline of its shape and the name of the instrument labeled inside the shape. The largest non-pitched instruments (those too big to fit on the table) I label on both the wall next to where it is located and the instrument itself.

Ethnic instruments are grouped together when space allows. I ensure that each instrument has its own label that indicates its country or region of origin (both on the instrument and where it is stored). Mallet containers (usually large cans) have labels for mallets for barred instruments and mallets for non-pitched instruments.

Materials for dance, drama, and movement (scarves, hoops, ribbon sticks, and so on) are grouped, located together, and labeled. So are CDs, DVDs, sheet music, and even textbooks.

Writing materials and everything associated with notation (paper, pencils, staff paper, whiteboards, erasers, erasable pens, crayons, small sticks for rhythmic notation, note heads for melodic notation) are grouped together and labeled, and each has its own specific location, also labeled.

When it is time to use a musical instrument or any other classroom item, I call a student's number (fairly, using a spinner) and tell the student what to get for his or her team. After the teams complete their task, the same numbered students who got the items put the items back in the same place where they found them. After a couple of times, this efficient method of getting things and putting them back becomes the understood rule in the classroom.

At the beginning of the school year, I spend a lot of time explaining the location of each of these items and also what I expect when the items are put away:

- Placing paper in neat piles
- Laying things in boxes and cans gently
- Taking care of all the materials so that other students will have them to use next time
- Placing mallets "heads up," instead of carelessly tossing the mallets into the cans
- Walking to the specific location where an item is kept, and not crowding in front of one another
- Saying "Excuse me" as a polite and socially acceptable way to behave

A teacher should not assume that good behaviors are already habitual in the children. These good behaviors must be explained, modeled, and practiced.

Again, a skeptic might think that teaching how the classroom is organized and how to take care of things takes time away from teaching music, but good behaviors will make your music making in the classroom much more enjoyable. At the beginning of every new school year, I dedicate an introductory lesson to teach my classroom expectations. You need not go through all your expectations in every lesson, but reminding your students what you expect of them when necessary will pay dividends in future music-making. I always tell my students, "I am a teacher first and a music teacher second."

Dividing into Groups

One of the most difficult tasks for the teacher in cooperative learning classrooms is deciding how to group students. You have an extraordinary number of personality variables to weigh: heterogeneous/homogeneous groups, introverted/extroverted personalities, high academically/low academically, musical/non-musical, popular/ unpopular, gender, race, culture, religion, aggressive behavior, bully- ing, and so on.

At the beginning of each school year, you may not know the students, so you might need to group them randomly. Conferring with other classroom teachers is a good idea throughout the year, but initially they won't know their students either. If you know some students from prior years, you can group them randomly but with some caveats. Watch out for students with a history of behavioral problems and those who tend to be argumentative. If two argumentative students are in the same group, you might be asking for problems. While it is important for students to know how to get along with each other regardless of their behavior, it is better to avoid confrontational groupings until everyone in your class has the opportunity to work on cooperative behavior.

Teams containing only boys or only girls usually work together well, but my experience is that boy teams generally work together better. Grade-school-age all-girl teams sometimes might gang up on one another. Girls within a group might pick on one member of the group, or two girls might be such good friends that they ignore the others in the team. Be sure that you know your students' personalities as well as possible before you put them into teams.

If your classes have an imbalance of boys and girls, sometimes you cannot avoid having a team with only one girl or one boy in the mix. This can work if the single student has a strong feeling of self-worth. In my school, most teachers are women, and I explain to my students that the male teachers work together really well with the women despite there being fewer of them. Having teams of good teachers to model really helps student teams.

It is of the utmost importance to know your students. To learn more about them, confer with their classroom teachers who spend more time with them than you. However, since you specifically teach music, keep in mind your students' musical abilities as well as their academic skills when you put them into teams.

The more organized you are at the beginning, the easier your record keeping will be throughout the year. Once you have a system in place, you will feel less stress and have more accurate records for each team, student, and class. After you organize, you are now ready to set the stage for making music with your students.

CHAPTER FOUR

SETTING THE STAGE

In today's society, politeness, sharing, kindness, listening, and positive conflict resolution have virtually disappeared from many homes. All too often, my young students seem not to know these valuable social skills. Perhaps the loss of these skills stems from too much screen time in front of computers, video games, and television. Or perhaps today's parents work so hard to make ends meet that they don't have time to teach these skills. While it is hard to say why these social skills seem to be almost non-existent with some students, I feel that it is my responsibility as a teacher to teach these skills. I believe that part of being a teacher is to make the world a better place. But, when I began teaching cooperative learning, I naively thought that all children already knew these social skills. Although my first experiences with cooperative learning were fraught with problems, I evaluated the problems and came up with some solutions.

Preparing the Students

Politeness

In order to teach politeness in my music classroom, I put up a sign saying: "This is a please and thank you station." Students asked me what the sign meant. I told them that if I heard anyone say "please," they would get a ticket to enter a drawing for a prize at the end of the month. Likewise, any time I heard a "thank you," I would give that person a drawing ticket. At first, I received many "thank yous" whenever I handed out instruments or other musical equipment to the students. But what I hoped to hear was "please" and "thank you" among the students themselves in their teams—and when I heard that, I pointed it out to the whole class and rewarded it. That led to lots of kind language. After a few classes, I didn't give out tickets every time, but only randomly. Sometimes a student would say "thank you" to me and I would say merely "you're welcome" without giving him or her any ticket. When they asked why they didn't get a ticket, I told them, "Even though you might not always get a ticket when you say 'please' or 'thank you,' continue to say those kind words because you might be rewarded with a ticket—but mostly because it feels good to be polite." My goal was to create politeness slowly and gradually without an extrinsic reward. Later, I began to hear students say such things to each other as "please go get me my mallets" without any extrinsic reward. Politeness didn't happen immediately, but as I kept reinforcing the word "please" with verbal reminders and tickets, polite conversation eventually emerged. But still, someone might forcefully say, "Get me my mallets!" And whenever I heard impoliteness, I would stop to remind the students how they sounded by exaggeratedly echoing their impolite statement and mimicking their forceful voice—but always tactfully. The students would laugh and then rephrase their statements with a "please" and a kinder voice. This all took time, but was well worth the effort.

SHARING

In cooperative learning, students need to share. And a great way to introduce the concept of sharing is using a "talking stick." In earlier lessons I already had enforced sharing using spinners with numbers or colors on them (see page 24), but I wanted to teach the students to share between themselves spontaneously with no help from me. I wanted to teach them to share within their teams independently in a happy way. So I decided to play a game using a "talking stick," which is simply a stick that serves as a symbol to allow the student who holds it to be the only one in the team who talks. (Actually, we used special sticks with wooden animals on top— it made talking sticks more special.) I found pictures of different tasks in educational books, and distributed one picture to each team. Then I asked the teams how they thought the task in the picture should be accomplished. They were to take the "talking stick" and pass it around the team members, speaking only when they held the stick. The job of the other students was to listen to the ideas of the person holding the stick. (Listening needs to be taught, too. See page 47.) After every student in the team had had a turn with the "talking stick" to discuss the picture, they were to put the stick down on their team letter so I knew the team was done. When all the teams had finished their discussions, I spun a spinner to select one person from each team to be the team's spokesperson, and I spun again to select which team would share its ideas first. Every team spokesperson mentioned the word "sharing."

This was a great opportunity for me to ask the students what the word "share" meant to them. Most felt it meant to take turns equally. Then we discussed how they could take turns equally in their teams. They came up with a number of ways to share. At first they thought it was best to go in order of the numbers they had been assigned within their teams, but then they considered that that was not always fair because number one would always get to go first. They decided it was fairer to let each person have a chance to go first at some point during the music lesson. We also talked about how much time was fair for each person's turn to speak (or to do any task). They decided everyone should have the same amount of time, and that either the teacher or someone in the team could keep track of the time using a timer.

Our discussion about sharing took most of the music lesson, but I wanted them to practice what they discovered, so I gave them the simple task of playing a made-up melody on a pitched instrument of their team's choice. I wanted to see if they would apply what they had discovered through their discussion of sharing. The task was a huge success! Before the teams began to play their melodies, they decided that the teacher should be the timer for each melody player, and the teams determined the order of the players by themselves. Success!

KINDNESS

I've watched students forcefully grab mallets out of one another's hands. I've heard students respond to my ideas with, "That's stupid." I've seen students push each other to try to force each other to move a certain way that they didn't want to. These examples of aggressive unkindness are best addressed *before* they happen. Role-playing helps greatly to reinforce the kinder way to handle these situations. However, even though it's better to teach role-playing with kindness before any situation escalates to pushing and shoving, role-playing can be a very effective teaching moment immediately afterwards.

To teach kindness using role-playing, set up scenarios for teams to perform in two ways: a rude way and a kind way to behave. Write several scenarios on pieces of paper, and let each team select a scenario at random. Here is one example scenario: "In a task where students suggest movements to add to a dance, one student suggests a dance motion that no one else likes." From that example scenario, a team should create two resolutions: How would you respond to the idea rudely? How would you respond to the idea kindly? Act this out. Each team then shares its scenario with the class, and everyone discusses.

Most students soon understand how to approach each other in a gentler and kinder way. But sometimes you might have to suggest kind phrases to the students if they are having a difficult time finding a thoughtful solution for a task. With patience and in time, students will be able to find kind solutions on their own. It helped me to write out these examples of kind language on a poster that I mounted on the wall:

- "That's a good idea, but let's hear some others."
- "Let's vote on that and see what happens."
- "Thank you for your creation."
- "You are doing a good job contributing."
- "We haven't heard from '(insert name).'"
- "Let's put that idea on hold."
- "Maybe we can combine that idea with another?"

LISTENING

"How do we listen?" is an important question to discuss with your students. They might have learned their own ideas about what listening means from their own individual classroom teachers, but in a cooperative learning classroom we will need to reinforce and expand these ideas. Even adults often could use some advice on how to listen!

I tell my students that there are four important skills they must learn to be a good listener:

1. Look at the person talking. Watching attentively is polite and lets the person know that who they are and what they are saying are important to the listener.

2. Keep your mouth closed. If you are talking, you can neither hear nor comprehend what the speaker is saying.

3. Sit very still. If you fidget, you cannot really focus on what is being said.

4. Think about what the person is saying. If you are not thinking about what the person is saying, you can have all of the above skills, but you will not really be taking in what is being said.

Once again, I list these skills on a poster that I hang in the classroom and review almost daily, especially during any time we share ideas.

During times I expect the students to listen to music, whether music shared by the teacher or made by other students, there usually are particular aspects of the music for which to listen. I write these particular aspects on the board. Perhaps I want the students to listen for a particular musical form (like A–B–A), for whether the performance is precise or sloppy, whether specific musical elements can be distinguished (such as dynamics, tempi, legato, staccato or whatever the concept is), whether the performers are enjoying themselves, or whether each student as a listener enjoyed the performance. Was the music interesting? Did it seem to have enough contrast, but some repetition? Did it include a surprise or a "twist"? These are specific musical aspects the students can listen for as audience members or make happen as performers. To make the listening active, students always need to have things to listen for—for example, I might ask them to gesture with a particular motion whenever they hear a recurrent musical motive. Students learn best when they are actively involved during their listening, either listening to a person speak or listening to music being performed.

Conflict Resolution

There have been many books written on conflict resolution, and many describe common situations that are prevalent in cooperative learning groups. Common conflicts include: arguing because someone always gets his or her way and the other person never gets his or hers; being upset because one team member doesn't work or contribute to the team; one person trying to run the whole team; and finally, an even number of team members competing for their ideas against an equal number of others without ever coming to a resolution.

At times, situations might escalate to physical conflict (especially over sharing items), but this rarely happens because I constantly monitor the teams. This physically aggressive behavior is never tolerated, and anyone involved is removed immediately to a time-out. If the behavior is severe enough, any students in question are sent to the principal's office, and I recommend calling home that day. I have found that physical conflicts often are due to differences between students' backgrounds, or (very commonly) an ongoing bad relationship between two students. If you catch physical conflicts as they are about to happen, you can explore their potential to be teachable moments. Through role-playing, scenarios, and discussion in teams and with the whole class, you gradually can eliminate most aggressive behavioral problems. Students will begin to realize that even adults might not get along with everyone, but we always need to deal with our differences in civilized ways, never with physical or verbal violence.

Strategies that my students have recommended to resolve conflicts include: the rock, paper, scissors game; flipping a coin (I always have one on a "coin spot" on my desk); voting; compromising; or beginning again if a team has time. All of these can be great solutions to conflicts, and it is common during the middle of a class for a team member to grab the coin on my desk and ask me to flip for the team to make their final decision.

Arguing

It is important to have ways to help students with different opinions be heard before a quiet discussion turns into a shouting match. Using talking sticks (see page 45) is a great way for everyone to get the opportunity to speak without interruption. Another useful strategy is taking turns with tokens. Each student starts with the same number of tokens, and the team sits around the team letter. When one student places a token onto the team letter, he or she may speak, and when that student's marker has been used, he or she must listen to the others. Both the talking stick and using tokens are fair ways for each student to have their voice heard. Once the students have shared their ideas, they need to discuss which ones they prefer. A democratic vote is one way to decide which idea to use. But if one person's ideas are constantly voted down, it is the job of the team to make sure everyone shares fairly so that each person gets his or her idea used during the day's lesson. The teacher must continually discuss and model compromise, because "compromise" is a concept that many students have rarely experienced. Students will gradually learn to compromise by combining their ideas, or using one idea and then adding another on top of it, or by using parts of many different ideas.

Working Equally

When a student consistently does not perform his or her equal part within the team, the others in the team have a huge problem. When one team member becomes disengaged, we tactfully discuss with the whole class how shyness or laziness might contribute to an unfair situation. Most of the time, role-playing with shy or lazy behaviors helps students recognize the difference between the two. Through seeing other students in these roles or exaggerating these roles themselves, students who unknowingly display these kinds of behaviors often come to realize they are, in fact, behaving in that way. Done with tact, many times shy or lazy people come around and contribute really amazing ideas. And that makes them less shy and lazy.

Unfortunately, trying to motivate a student with persistent lazy behavior can be extraordinarily difficult for a teacher or a parent, and even more difficult for student peers. Generally, if the unmotivated student is included in a team of overly assertive students, he or she relies on the team's work and remains unmotivated. On the other hand, if the unmotivated student is included in a team of other unmotivated students, the entire team's quality of results is usually poor. I have found that including an unmotivated student with average students produces the best results. And, including one outstanding student within that team often helps all of the team members be more motivated to produce better results. Extrinsic rewards (such as tickets, candy treats, or trinkets for the most outstanding team's result) sometimes motivate the less-motivated student. I would rather use intrinsic rewards (like feeling good for a job well done), but if I know it will work I will use extrinsic rewards to motivate a disengaged student.

HOW TO GET THE JOB DONE

A poster in my music room has the title "How to Get the Job Done." The poster lists these ways to get the job done:

- Listen.
- Share.
- Make decisions in a timely fashion.
- Practice until it's good.

I can't emphasize enough how vital it is for you as a teacher to be a good model to show your students these four steps. Listening and sharing will drastically improve when students practice (and you model) the methods described earlier in this chapter. But frequently, the most difficult of the four steps is "make decisions in a timely fashion." Taking too long with decisions takes time away from practicing, and often the end results are mediocre or poor. We discuss quality of work and how many times the team needs to practice a task before the result is good. My students usually tell me that it takes from three to five practices before they feel a task can be considered good, but I tell them, "Practice as many times as it takes to make the task really good in the eyes of each team member." Teams soon find out the hard way what it's like to give a poor performance when the time comes for sharing and they are not ready because they did not allow enough time for practice.

After teams start to master the techniques of cooperative learning, students will have many ideas to share, but making decisions in a cooperative manner can be difficult. It is important that the teacher ensures that the teams are moving at the right pace in order to complete their task successfully. I walk around and observe the teams to see how far along they are in their tasks, and I remind them how much time they have left to finish. If I see they are falling behind, I help them make decisions to speed up their task. Or, if they need my help, I might offer to put together some of their ideas. Sometimes they accept my help, but other times they refuse and say they want to decide quickly for themselves. At first, the teacher is responsible to keep each team on task and on time. But as your journey with cooperative learning continues, getting the job done on time will become more and more the responsibility of each team. Team autonomy is your ultimate goal.

Chapter Five

Team-Building Activities

Taking a few moments in each lesson to build team loyalty pays off in the long term big time. And the more loyal the students are to their team, the more likely their tasks will be successful and of high quality. In short, when student's hearts are invested in their work, they will produce a better "product" and increase their cooperation. Students with surface differences soon realize that they have more in common than they ever expected, but also that their differences make each individual more interesting.

The Importance of Loyalty, Acceptance, and Conflict Resolution

I start most of my lessons with a short team-building activity to help instill a sense of teamwork and loyalty. Some activities help teammates get to know each other better. Other activities foster healthy competition between the teams so that members of each team develop trust and camaraderie. But I find that the best results come from team-building activities that are brief and don't take time away from making music or teaching bigger concepts.

Following are many team-building activities that have proven successful for me during my many years of teaching. I encourage you to create your own team-building activities and to share the activities you find to be particularly successful with your colleagues. Team-building activities, in addition to being an imaginative way to begin any music class, will bring immediate enthusiasm to your lesson.

- **Team naming**—Let each team decide on a team name. To point your students in the right direction, you might attach a theme to the names (for example, composers, instruments, music groups, or whatever). Limit the time for this activity to less than three minutes.

- **Team handshake**—Let each team decide on a special team handshake so that, when a team has succeeded in a task that is done well, they have a way of acknowledging their success together. The handshake must involve every person in the team, not just pairs. Time limit for this activity should be under five minutes.

- **Team color**—Let each team decide on a team color. This might encourage them to wear clothes with their team color on days that they have music class. Time limit for this activity should be under three minutes.

- **Team special movement**—Let each team decide on a special movement for their team (a brief dance step, salute, wave, etc.). Time limit for this activity should be under five minutes. Then, the first thing each team can do upon entering the classroom is their special team movement. (Perhaps, on a day you're teaching musical forms and dance, each team could use their movement as an A-section to a "movement rondo."

- **Puzzles of the rules**—Give each team an envelope containing a thick piece of paper on which is written all the rules for the classroom but cut up into puzzle shapes. Give each team five minutes to put the puzzles together without speaking. Whichever team correctly completes the task first gets tickets for a monthly prize drawing.

- **Naming non-pitched instruments**—woods, metals, skins—Give each team a pencil and a piece of paper on a clipboard. At a given signal, without talking, each team passes the pencil and paper on the clipboard around and writes down the names of non-pitched percussion instruments from the "wood" family (for example, claves). At the "time's up" signal, the team that correctly wrote down the most wooden non-pitched instruments wins tickets for a monthly prize drawing. On another day, play the same game writing down non-pitched metals (or on yet another day, skins). The time limit for this activity should be under ten minutes.

- **Naming pitched instruments**—bass xylophone, alto metallophone, etc.—Play the same game as the non-pitched instrument game above, except name pitched instruments instead.

- **Round Robin competition**—Really, any game, either written or spoken, in which each team member gets to take equal turns to contribute to complete a whole task. Round Robins are rather like brainstorming. Each team sits in a circle, and one team member takes one turn at a time. If a team member cannot think of anything when it is his or her turn, he or she passes the turn to the next team member. For example, pass a piece of paper and pencil around the circle. Each team member quickly writes down an idea or answer (whatever you instruct them to do) and then passes the paper and pencil on to the next team member. It is important for the teacher to underscore that if the team member with the paper and pencil cannot think of an idea or answer, then it is better just to pass his or her turn to the next person in the circle. Passing one turn might give that student time to think of an idea or answer when the paper and pencil come around again in the next turn.

- **Find similarities with or without speaking**—Given less than three minutes, team members discover what they all have in common. The team that discovers the most things in common shares what they found with the whole class. This can be anything from eye color to favorite pizza toppings, and can be done with or without talking. Doing this activity without talking is very challenging and might take longer, but it's a whole lot of fun!

- **Team drawing**—Draw a picture on a whiteboard with each team member having only one chance to contribute to the drawing, rather like round robin, done without talking. This team activity should take less than two minutes and could be tied in with a particular song you will be introducing, for example: "Draw a flower garden...Ready, set, go!"

- **Create a team saying**—Let each team decide on its favorite saying, phrase, or motto. You may want to attach a theme to the team saying, such as kindness, school rules, important things to remember, etc. Limit the time for this activity to less than five minutes.

QUICK TEAM BUILDING

The following quick team-building activities should last only three minutes. However, make sure that each team member has had a chance to contribute. Activities with tight time limits teach students how to share in the few moments that they have together. A common pitfall during these quick tasks happens when one team member takes up all the time and the rest of the teammates don't get their chance to contribute. But after a few quick tasks, the students will learn that they need to manage their brief time wisely. After the teams learn about efficient time management through these quick team-building activities, they will be able to apply their efficiency skills later to longer and more important tasks, and their results will be more successful.

- • Discover a food that everyone in your team likes.
- • Discover a TV program that everyone in your team likes.
- • Discover a music group that everyone in your team likes.
- • Discover a music group that everyone in your team *doesn't* like.
- • Share what pets you have and their names. (If you don't have a pet, share one you wish you had and its name.)
- • Tell your teammates about your family.
- • Tell your teammates your favorite place to travel.

A team-building activity at the start of each lesson helps to create team trust, loyalty, familiarity, shared experiences, anticipation for the lesson, and fun. Also, short team-building activities make great transition times for you as a teacher. Your music schedule might move so rapidly or might be so full of ideas, or perhaps you struggle changing pace from working with kindergarteners to immediately working with sixth graders—a quick team-building activity gives you time to get your head prepared for the lesson while the teams spend productive time together. As they build team skills, students are actively involved and are getting ready to learn music.

CHAPTER SIX

TEACHING THROUGH MODELING

Having a good teacher to model greatly benefits students as they work on regular projects and especially on cooperative learning projects. Oftentimes, without a model, students will misunderstand what a task entails and will produce unexpected results. Normally in my lessons, I do a task first as a "try-out" with the whole class, and I answer any questions and obtain their input before I give the "go-ahead" to split into teams to begin their own projects. Often, I demonstrate with a project that I completed beforehand to show the students the process they will need to use in order to be successful in their teams. However, whenever I model, afterwards I encourage the students to employ their own ideas and not simply copy my creations. But if I ever see a team struggling to come up with ideas, I might suggest that they begin with part of my idea and add their own ideas to it to make it their own.

When I model, I review the process for each task thoroughly to make sure students fully understand their task. Usually I write the steps required for a team to be successful on the board as I demonstrate. But for some tasks I write the steps on a piece of paper, which I copy and distribute to each team. It helps immensely for a teacher to assign one member of the team to be the "process-reminder" in order to keep the team on track. (Another job! See page 18.)

Also, I have found it very useful to write down how much time should be spent for each part of the process. During the task, I facilitate by going from team to team to remind them how far along they should be as time progresses. But, as the teams get better at working together, they also will get better at managing their time. They might run out of time at first, but soon they will make sure they have enough time to complete their project, especially if the task requires time to practice to share their work in front of the whole class.

It's amazing to watch how modeling works. For example, I'll teach the entire class a melody that each team will alter to fit the concept I wish to reinforce. Then, in teams each teammate makes sure every team member is able to play the melody successfully before the team changes it. The students get to experience being the teacher, which develops their confidence, autonomy, and self-esteem. I love to watch this happen—the team dynamics are always fascinating. I become so exhilarated when I see a timid student step out of his or her comfort zone and develop social skills by teaching others.

Once the team members trust each other, they can constructively criticize how well the team accomplished its task, the performance of each team member, and themselves.

A MODELING EXAMPLE

Here is how I would model a lesson where teams will create a three-note melody with "sol, mi, la" and the Curwen hand signs. I would teach this lesson after students already have had some experiences with "sol, mi, la" songs and using Curwen hand signs—for example, playing "sol, mi, la" songs on barred instruments, adding movement to these songs through play-parties, notating them on the board on a "three line staff" (when sol is a lineman, mi is a lineman; when sol is a spaceman, mi is a spaceman), and adding ostinati to these songs. After the students acquire basic skills, then the teams can create their own "sol, mi, la" songs.

Before the teams work on the task for themselves, I model the whole process for the entire class.

- The teacher sings and uses Curwen hand signs for a short "sol, mi, la" motive. The class echoes the song and the hand signs several times. Then the teacher writes the motive on the "three line staff."

- The teacher sings and uses Curwen hand signs for a *second* "sol, mi, la" motive. The class echoes the song and the hand signs. Then the teacher adds the second motive to the first on the "three line staff."

- The teacher sings and uses Curwen hand signs for a *third* "sol, mi, la" motive. The class echoes the song and the hand signs. Then the teacher adds the motive to the first two on the "three line staff."

- The teacher sings and uses Curwen hand signs for a *fourth* and final "sol, mi, la" motive. The class echoes the song and the hand signs. Then the teacher adds the motive to the other three on the "three line staff."

- The teacher asks the class, "How many motives did you hear?" (Four motives.) The teacher numbers each motive above the "three-line staff" 1, 2, 3, and 4.

- The class members choose their favorite motive of the four by a vote.

- The teacher writes the motive the class liked best three times on another "three line staff." This is the start of the new melody that the students get to finish.

- The teacher asks the students to think of a new final motive to end the new melody, practicing silently in their heads as they use Curwen hand signs.

- The teacher calls on a few students to hear the final motive they made up. (You don't need to spend too much time now. Remember this is just the model session for practice—the teams will do this themselves in a few minutes.) The class listens to a few final motives and then decides which one they like best. The teacher writes it down on the "three-line staff" after the three motives that start the melody.

- The class sings and uses Curwen hand signs for their completed new melody.

- The teacher asks the class to play the new melody using barred instruments.

We're not ready to start the task in teams yet. First we must review the whole process on how to make the "sol, mi, la" melody step by step and discuss how much time they might expect to spend on each step. Explain the objective clearly: create a "sol, mi, la" melody that has four motives, three motives should be the same and the final motive should be different. They should be able to sing the melody, use Curwen hand signs for it, and learn how to play it on barred instruments. At the end of the lesson, the members of each team should perform their melody by singing it and using hand signs, and then play the melody on their instruments. Underscore ways how each team member can share his or her ideas before the team decides which motives they like best. Once your discussion has concluded, make sure the teams have the materials they need (paper and pencils to write out "three-line staffs" and their motives). Then give the teams your signal to begin their project. As the teams work, the teacher needs to facilitate the time and make sure each team is moving toward a decision efficiently. The teams must leave enough time to practice for their performance. After a team has written down their melody, they can get their instruments and mallets. Remind them to use *six-inch voices* and play their instruments with *six-inch sounds* (see page 26), ensure they know how to "get the job done" (as your poster shows, see page 52), and that sharing and kindness are important (see page 47).

When working in teams on a creative project, big egos often come to the forefront. To create a healthy learning environment, review as many cooperative skills as you need to before you set the teams off on their task. Good teaching will address both a special cooperative skill and a musical concept. For our example, perhaps the cooperative skill on which to work is "listens to the ideas of others." Writing the skill on a "sentence strip" to post on the board will remind the team members about the cooperative skill needed for the task at hand. But, you should highlight the cooperative skill that needs the most work in your classroom.

CHAPTER SEVEN

TAKING OFF

EVALUATION

Every day, I keep track of how well my students perform their musical skills, how well they develop cooperative skills, and how well they behave. From my records, I can see how everyone progresses over the whole year, from month to month, and day by day. Our school has nine-week grading periods, and I use my records to calculate a grade for each student for music class on their report cards.

I keep track of each of my three categories for evaluation (musical skills, cooperative skills, and behavior) on different colored sheets of paper. That way I can tell them apart easily, and they are easier to find when I need to fill them in with my notes or when I read through them as I assemble my grades.

MUSICAL SKILLS EVALUATION SHEETS

Before the start of each school year, I create a musical skills evaluation sheet for each of my classes. Each musical skills sheet covers one calendar month. I write the month on the top right side, along with the class and grade-level. And, down the left side of the page, I list the skills that I will teach during the month. I have one grade book for each of my classes with one of these pages for each month. I leave plenty of room to write names, make notes about the students, and quickly rate student musical skills on a scale from 1 to 5, with 1 being the lowest and 5 being the most outstanding. My notes help immensely when the time comes to assign a grade to each student at the end of our nine-week grading period. When I need to make comments to parents or other teachers, I can easily assemble what I need from my notes. I am also able to review my students' progress month by month throughout the school year and note their improvement.

Musical Skills Evaluation Sheet

Month: _____
Class: _____
Grade: _____

Skills for the Month:

Eighth note durations:

Sixteenth note durations:

Pentatonic singing "so, mi, la":

Improvisation:

COOPERATIVE SKILLS EVALUATION SHEETS

In addition to my musical skills evaluation sheet, I prepare a sheet for each month that lists the cooperative learning skills I will teach. The cooperative skills sheets look similar to the musical skills sheets, but I print them on different colored paper so I can tell them apart easily. Instead of musical skills, I list cooperative skills on the left side of the page. Again, I leave plenty of room to write down student names, notes, and what I observe.

Cooperative Skills Evaluation Sheet

Month: _____
Class: _____
Grade: _____

- Invites others to contribute
- Maintains eye contact with teammates
- Uses a quiet voice or instrument in order to be respectful of others
- Praises other teammates and other students
- Checks with teacher for understanding
- Able to disagree in an agreeable way
- Listens to the ideas of others
- Focuses on the task at hand
- Takes turns
- Shares (ideas, equipment, etc.)
- Takes suggestions
- Accepts criticism
- Works equally in the team
- Compromises in a polite manner
- Says "please" and "thank you"
- Uses time wisely
- Able to make decisions in a timely manner

BEHAVIOR EVALUATION SHEETS

My behavioral evaluation sheets, once again, are on a different color paper than the musical skills sheets or the cooperative skills sheets for identification purposes. At the top of the behavioral evaluation sheet, I write the class and grade-level. Under this title I write headings under which I can record the date when any behavioral problem occurred, who was involved, what happened, and what the consequences were.

Behavioral Evaluation Sheet

Month: _____
Class: _____
Grade: _____

Date	Name	Infraction	Consequence

Again, I can fill this sheet in quickly when one class is leaving my classroom and the next is entering. Keeping precise records of student behavior gives you a documented list of details to refer to if it ever is necessary to make a phone call to a parent or if a parent calls you with questions about how their child is behaving.

You can also use the information you record in your sheets to determine a student's grade for behavior, depending on the number of times a student's name appears on your list. If a student's name never appears on the behavioral evaluation sheet, he or she receives an "O" for outstanding. If a student's name is on the list just one or two times, he or she receives an "S" for satisfactory. But if a student's name appears on the list more than twice during the nine-week grading period, he or she receives an "N" for needs improvement.

(Your school might have a standardized behavior grading plan. Adjust your grading system to your needs.) But you don't want to surprise anyone with an unexpected grade. At the beginning of the school year, send out letters telling the parents the grading system you intend to use. Clear communication with the parents is crucial.

Summary

In my music classes, each student receives a grade for musical skills, a grade for cooperative learning skills, and a behavior grade. (Combining the cooperative learning and behavior evaluations into one grade also works well.) In my experience, students with outstanding musical skills also have outstanding cooperative learning skills and behavior. However, sometimes a student with outstanding musical skills has difficulties in other areas. You also will find students who are polite and cooperative but simply have less musical talent and understanding. That's why I believe it is important not to combine evaluations of these categories for a single grade. As music teachers, our principle job is to teach musical skills. Even if a student misbehaves, it does not mean he or she cannot sing in tune, improvise like a wizard, or move like a lynx. An excellent musician deserves an outstanding musical grade, and behavior should not enter into any evaluation of musical skills or conceptual understanding. However, to help the child who has behavioral problems improve (and to make your class more enjoyable for everyone), the parents need to know that their child needs to improve his or her social skills. I reiterate: we are teachers first, music teachers second. We have a social duty to nurture kindness, thoughtfulness, and understanding in our students so that, through the arts, we might more readily achieve peace.

CHAPTER EIGHT

TYPES OF COOPERATIVE LEARNING STRUCTURES

Other books on cooperative learning describe many different methods to structure cooperative learning classrooms. However, some structural methods serve the active music-making classroom better than others. In this chapter, I'll explain many cooperative learning structures that I have used with success in my music classroom:

- Puzzles
- Think—Pair—Share and Think—Pair—Squared—Share
- Inside—Outside Circle
- Roundtable
- Three-Step Interview
- Circle of Knowledge
- Send a Problem
- Numbered Heads Together
- Jigsaw
- Game Activities

These structures are most successful when your teaching addresses both musical skills and cooperative skills simultaneously. And, it's important to assess your efforts so that you can see how well you and your students are doing, and can chart paths for improvement. (See chapter 9.)

PUZZLES

You can use this cooperative learning structure with from two to six students in a team, however, two, three, or four work best. Hand out a puzzle to each team (perhaps through one team member in charge of materials). Set a time limit in which the teams need to solve their puzzles as quickly as possible. If the team correctly solves the puzzle in time, each member of the team gets a point. But if the team doesn't finish or if their puzzle wasn't solved correctly, they don't get any points. Whichever team has the most points at the end of the time limit gets a reward (whatever you determine would motivate them). The puzzles could expand on concepts you've taught them recently, or perhaps the puzzles could review concepts that they learned earlier in the year. Using puzzles is also a great way to prepare for a test. Healthy competition between teams is fun and encourages team members to work together harder.

THINK—PAIR—SHARE

Using this structure, team members first take time to think of a solution for a problem by themselves individually, next team members pair with one another to work together, and finally the pairs share their ideas with the whole team. First the teacher presents a problem, such as how to end the teacher's unfinished rhythmic phrase. Ask the students to think of a solution by themselves individually. After a few minutes, ask the students to pair with someone they are sitting close to and share their solutions. You might decide that simply sharing is what you want to teach. But, you could choose to have the pair compromise their solutions and come up with one solution to present as a pair to the whole team. A compromise might entail adding each person's rhythms together in their entirety, or using a part of each of the rhythms and combining them to create one new rhythm. Or perhaps the compromise might be that the pair begins all over again with a new rhythm. The pairs then share their rhythms with the whole team. Depending on the team's experience with compromising and their grade level, you can expand this structure to *Think—Pair—Squared—Share*. The "squared" part means to expand the structure by adding a step where, after the pairs present their solutions to the team, the team again takes aspects of the solutions that the pairs came up with, and through compromise, assembles their own team solution. Because Think—Pair—Squared—Share requires lots of compromise, it's best to reserve this structure for older students who have had many cooperative learning experiences.

INSIDE—OUTSIDE CIRCLE

In this cooperative learning structure, the class forms two concentric circles, each facing one another, then each person in the inside circle partners with a person in the outside circle. Ask either the *inside* or the *outside* person of each pair to present a problem of your choosing to his or her partner, and then the partner comes up with a solution. Then, select a spokesperson who shares the pair's solution with the whole class. Next, the students get new partners: one circle stays stationary and the other circle moves around until the teacher calls "halt." At that point, the inside and outside people who face each other partner up, and you present the problem again (or a new one) for the new partners to come up with a solution.

Continue using this structure as many times as you feel it continues to be effective. For variety, change which circle presents the problem and which circle comes up with the solution.

ROUNDTABLE

This structure is an activity for teams that can also be used for team-building. Give a piece of paper and a pencil to the "materials person" in each team. The team sits in a circle. The teacher spins to decide which team member will begin writing. No talking is permitted during the activity, or the team is disqualified. The teacher then presents a problem that can have many answers, and the writing begins. Each team member writes down an answer to the problem and passes the paper to the next team member in the circle. If a team member cannot come up with an answer, he or she passes the paper to the next person in the circle. (Let the students know it is okay to pass the paper and pencil if a student cannot think of an answer or idea at the moment. The point is to write down as many ideas as possible within the time limit. Remind them they are working together as a team, and if a student passes on one turn, when the paper and pencil comes around again he or she may have come up with a great idea.) The moment the teacher calls "time," whoever is writing drops the pencil and all hands go on the students' heads. The "materials person" gathers the pencil and paper with all the answers and returns them to the teacher for assessment.

THREE-STEP INTERVIEW

In this cooperative learning structure, the teacher gives an answer to one member of the team secretly; the rest of the team members do not know the answer. Each team member then asks the member who knows the answer a question that can be answered by "yes" or "no." When someone in the team guesses the correct answer, the teacher gives another team member another secret answer, and the interviewing continues. Even adults use this structure! Have you ever gone to a party where, as you walk through the door, the hostess assigns each guest a name of a famous person, but you do not know who that person is, and you must go around to all the other guests and ask questions that illicit a "yes or no" response in order to figure out which famous person you are? A hostess often plays this game as a mixer to warm up the party and to get people to visit with each other. The cooperative learning structure works similarly, except that each student stays within his or her team to find out the solution he or she is trying to discover.

Incidentally, the Three-Step Interview structure works best if the teacher models the proper behavior beforehand. I model both the ways to ask "yes or no" questions and how to speak at the proper volume level. When I role-model "yes or no" questions, I begin by asking more general questions about large concepts, and then ask more and more specific questions to demonstrate the technique for narrowing down to precise ideas in order to get to an answer more quickly than just random guessing. It's paramount to demonstrate *six-inch* voices or the class will get too loud and defeat your intended result. Demonstrating the proper way to speak within the distance of *six inch* voices, *across the room* voices, or *outside on the playground* voices is important not only for this activity, but for many cooperative learning activities. (See page 26.) It is fun to demonstrate by mixing the volumes up and getting the students giggling. But make sure that they know the serious consequences of speaking at an inappropriate volume level when actively engaged in any activity. I always stop any Three-Step Interview if the students do not abide with the *six-inch* voice rule. The *six-inch* volume also applies to the dynamic level they use when they play instruments.

Circle of Knowledge

In this structure, the teams each solve separate problems secretly, and afterwards they present their solution to the other teams as new problems to solve. First, the teacher presents each team with a separate problem to solve within a limited time. The teams must be very quiet as they work toward their solutions to ensure that the other teams don't overhear their secrets. The teams each write down their solution (or, depending on the problem, come up with another method to present their solution, such as a performance). When all the teams are ready, each team presents its solution to the other teams, who observe the solution, confer among themselves, and come up with their own response or answer. Then, each team selects a spokesperson to share that team's answer with the whole class.

Send a Problem

With this cooperative learning structure, the teams each solve the same problem that the teacher gives them within a limited amount of time and shares its solution with the class. Before they begin, discuss the way the team should solve the problem, how the team should decide its solution, and the way the team will present its solution (for example, will they write it down or perform it?). When all the teams have come up with their solutions to the problem, each team presents its solution to the entire class, which observes the solution and responds to it.

The "Send a Problem" structure differs slightly from the "Circle of Knowledge" structure: in "Send a Problem" every team works on and comes up with a solution for the same problem, whereas in "Circle of Knowledge" each team works on its own different problem. But to limit the scope of the "Circle of Knowledge" structure, I confine the problems on which the teams work to the same general theme or topic.

Before you use the "Send a Problem" structure, I suggest that you review the subject matter that you intend to use this structure to reinforce. When you see that your students have grasped the concepts you intend to teach, you can proceed into the "Send a Problem" structure (and role-modeling how you expect the students to work on their task might be very helpful for them). As a teacher, I find "Send a Problem" is very useful because you can see how well the students retain what you taught them—it's a great structure to give you feedback on the efficacy of your teaching.

Numbered Heads Together

Each team member gets to be the leader in this cooperative learning structure. Start with each team sitting or standing in a circle so that each team member can see the others easily. Give the teams a problem, and each team member takes a turn to lead the rest of the team as it comes up with a solution. After each team member has had at least one turn to lead the team, and the team has as many solutions as it has leaders, the whole team puts their heads together to assemble the best parts of the various solutions into a final solution for the whole team to present to the class. For example, if the problem was to come up with a movement to accompany each phrase of a four-phrase song, the leader of the team would present his or her own repetitive movement, and the rest of the teammates would mirror the leader's motion for each phrase. Then, the team would select a new leader in the team to create entirely new motions for each of the four phrases of the song. This would continue until each team member had an opportunity to be the leader of the team. After everyone has led their team, the team members choose parts of all of the motions to combine into a final version that the whole team decides on as its solution. After the teams make their decisions through compromise, ensure that you give them plenty of time to practice their solution and then share it with a performance for the whole class.

Jigsaw

This is a cooperative learning structure that mixes up members from different teams into new groups for a time, and then reassembles the teams to come up with a final solution. First, I divide the students into new groups by sorting them by their number within their team; I send all the ones to assemble into a group in one corner of the room, all the twos in another, etc. Then I give each new group a piece of a jigsaw puzzle with two answers on it. I present everyone with a question, and the new groups decide if their jigsaw pieces have the answer to the question, or which of their answers fits best. Then they reassemble back into their regular teams, and using the jigsaw pieces, they discuss what they learned from their new groups. I ask the teams to create a final solution using the answers on the jigsaw puzzle pieces that correspond to the answers they discovered when they had been in their new groups. To complete the structure, every team shares their solution with the entire class.

Game Activities

When I want a fun way to reinforce concepts or strengthen the teams, I use a game activity. Games spur healthy competition, which makes them valuable methods to develop team spirit, loyalty, and interdependence. I explain many games that have proven successful for me in Suggested Lessons (see chapter 11). But I encourage you to develop many more of your own, keeping in mind that game activities always should be used to address your targeted objectives in both musical skills and cooperative skills simultaneously.

After students have learned about music and themselves through many cooperative learning structures, they will begin to feel much more comfortable with each other. They will come to know which structures they prefer for which kinds of tasks and which structures are best suited for their teammates to produce great results. And knowing what methods they learn best from will make it easier for you and your students to assess the progress in your music class.

CHAPTER NINE

STUDENT ASSESSMENT

Individual assessment can be very tricky in cooperative learning situations, especially when one team member who does not contribute to a team's solution to a problem causes the hard work of the other team members to result in a poor performance. A teacher can address this issue by assigning two assessment grades, one for musical skills and another for cooperative skills. Whatever the cooperative learning skill is for a particular activity, be sure to observe and note who in the teams is contributing and who is not. I use a computer spreadsheet program that lists the class, grade level, and the cooperative skills incorporated into each activity; and after each class session I assess the students using a brief rating system to quickly note who is doing what. I rate on a scale from "1" to "5," with "1" being the lowest and "5" being the most outstanding. Sometimes, because I have only a few minutes between classes, I might not have enough time to note all of the students' contributions. In that case, I only rate those students who truly excelled and those who performed poorly. Then, for those students who I did not give a rating to during the day, I assume they performed adequately and therefore I give them an average "3" rating when I fill in the scores for everyone at the end of the day. This quick method of grading is much easier than trying to find every student's name in a mad rush and putting a "3" rating next to it.

Music is an aural art, and I feel that written tests cannot adequately assess musical skill, so I don't use written tests very often. Instead, I assess student performance—whether it is singing, playing an instrument, or movement. Through performance, a student is able to demonstrate his or her conceptual understanding of a musical element and, of course, his or her skill at any musical endeavor. Several times each class period, I let the students know that I am continuously evaluating them, thus their work becomes more and more productive and consistent. When it matters to students how they perform, it matters to them how they work as individuals and in teams, and they improve throughout the year.

Oftentimes, I can assess individuals as they work in their teams. For example, if I want to assess everyone's ability to play a melody on an instrument, I assemble the students into their teams, where they become teachers to each other as they practice their melody as a team in preparation for a performance in front of the whole class. Then, during the performance, I can assess the team's performance as a whole, or I can call out individuals as soloists for parts of the pieces for assessment on how they play for themselves.

But even when I need to assess students individually, I use cooperative situations to prepare them for their individual tests. The advance preparation puts the students at ease and serves as an example for what I expect them to know for their individual tests. For example, if I want to test individual music dictation (where each student writes down the notes for a rhythm or melody that I play), I might use a competitive game where teams place small sticks next to each other to represent the durations of a rhythm using quarter notes, pairs of eighth notes, quarter rests, or whatever duration I am testing—popsicle sticks work well. (If you don't have sticks to make rhythms, you can write rhythms using pencil and paper just as well.) When each team has its materials and is ready, I clap or speak a rhythm (always counting out one measure of a steady beat first) and the teams each must come up with one solution together, placing their sticks to correctly represent the rhythm. I repeat the rhythm until they complete the dictation. When a team reaches a solution, the team's captain stands. Once the captain stands, no one in the team is permitted to touch the sticks. The first team to correctly solve the dictation gets five points, but if a team captain stands and their solution is not correct they get no points. The second team to solve the dictation gets four points, and so on. I repeat the rhythm until all the captains are standing. Then, I start again with another rhythm. After a pre-determined time limit, the game ends and whichever team has the most points, wins the game. After we play this game a number of times, the students are ready to be tested individually on rhythmic dictation.

The key to proper assessment is careful observation. It is imperative for the teacher to circulate among the teams to observe how the students interact as they work on the tasks you assign. It's vital to walk around as you teach in order to observe, listen to, and evaluate every one of your students. Music is often very difficult to assess because it happens in the moment and then is over, so you need to observe your students like a home-plate umpire without instant replay. But, it's crucial to observe both how students prepare and their final product to evaluate them fairly.

PRINCIPLES FOR ASSESSMENT

In music class, you will teach students how to judge musical quality, and also how to tactfully assess one another's music making.

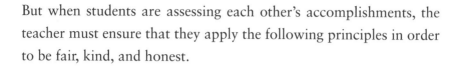

But when students are assessing each other's accomplishments, the teacher must ensure that they apply the following principles in order to be fair, kind, and honest.

- **Know what to listen for.**

  Any time students critique each other's performances, discuss beforehand what they should listen for. Come up with a list of things to listen for and assess during performance. That way the students will be active listeners. For example, if the students are performing a piece of music in a certain form, you might direct the students to ask: Were the players synchronized with each other? Did they play with expression? Was the performance interesting to hear and watch? Did they get right back on track after they made any mistakes?

- **Always show appreciation for effort and creativity through applause.**

  We should teach our students to appreciate everyone's sincere creative ideas, no matter what the level of achievement. By applauding, we show respect to others. We also show that we appreciate all the time and energy it took to come up with a creative solution.

- **Rate the performance.**

  After a performance, the audience should show its appreciation of the sincere effort of the performers with applause, and then should privately vote "one," "two," or "three" with their fingers at their chest level. When everyone's vote is private, only the teacher can see the rating and the other students cannot, so nobody will offend anyone else with their honest rating. A "one" vote is the very best and means that the performers followed the directions, performed with expression, and were synchronized with each other. A "one" vote also means that the audience member really enjoyed listening to or watching the performers. A "two" vote is an average score, and a "three" vote means that the student thought the performance was poor, off, didn't sound good, or missed the point of the directions.

- **Discuss why you rated the performance as you did.**

  After everyone has voted, the teacher asks a few of the students who rated the performance to give the reasons why they gave the rating they did (always with kindness and politeness). They must articulate "why" within the parameters of those things you directed them to listen for—not just because "I liked it." This gives immediate feedback to the performers, and also gives you a chance to direct the student's criticisms to guide the performers in constructive ways to improve.

- **Know musical taste is subjective.**

  Explain to your students that some people really like certain pieces of art or music, and that other people might not like the same piece of art or music—but it's okay to have different opinions. However, it is important to try to understand *why* you like it or dislike it. When you are able to tell someone else the reasons that you like or dislike a piece of art or music, then you have achieved a deeper knowledge of the subject and perhaps can help others to understand what to like in that piece.

- **Give criticism and then another round of applause.**

  It's easy for students to take criticism personally, especially when heavy criticism in class is new to the students. Make it absolutely clear that any criticism they hear is of their performance and not of anyone as an individual. Criticism is easier for people to receive if an individual's name is not mentioned. Instead, generalize about people as members of a team. I do not permit my students to use names when they criticize each other. Instead, we always say, "One person was not as together as the others in the team." To finish, we applaud once again to recapture the positive post-performance feeling and instill momentum towards improvement next time.

- **Educate discriminating listeners.**

  It is our job to educate listeners who know how to judge artistic quality. Regretfully, much of the music that children listen to today is of poor quality. It is a vital component of our jobs as music educators to teach our students about good music in *every* genre—and to teach them what they need to listen for in those genres that makes the music good. Creating a discriminating musical audience will certainly help fill the concert halls of our orchestras, operas, and ballets in the future. In fact, if we don't train our children to love music, our artistic culture will shrivel, if it survives at all. And when good music is treasured by the broader society, public music education will be valued, rightfully, by school administrators and local communities, whose support is essential to safeguard school music programs in tough economic times.

- **Know and teach national standards.**

  As teachers, we need to be aware of all the National Standards for Music Education and teach them equally. Also remember that music is an aural art, not just a visual art—national music standards are only one-ninth about notation, the rest is about making music.

- **Know who your students will become.**

  Who your students become—music consumers, performers, audience members, ticket buyers, music downloaders, instrument purchasers, community chorus or instrumental ensemble members, future music teachers, directors, or conductors—is important for you as a teacher to ponder when you assess your students and create their music lessons. As teachers, we need to have realistic expectations of the people we teach. Very few of our students will become professional performers—or even music teachers—but many (maybe almost all) will make music a vital and meaningful part of their lives.

GRADING

Ultimately, fairly assessing music students involves only a handful of basic considerations: Did the student grow according to his or her musical abilities? Did the student contribute to the team cooperatively? Did the student's skills in cooperative learning grow? From the start (not after you send out report cards), it is important that both students and parents understand how you are assessing the individuals in your class. I give two grades at the end of our nine-week grading periods: one for musical skills (with comments) and the other for cooperative learning skills and behavior (with comments).

I reiterate: separate grades for musical and cooperative skills seem to provide a more accurate assessment than just a single grade. And, because assessment always involves—at least in part—a teacher's subjective opinions, I have found it most valuable for the students' long-term progress to use the grades "Outstanding," "Satisfactory," and "Needs Improvement" and write a paragraph or two of comments for each student to explain my grading. Grading this way helps guide students towards fully realizing their natural abilities in the longer term, whereas letter grades do not. Letter grades seem to stigmatize students and categorize them as a percentage or a number rather than recognize each of them as an individual. Also, parents seem to accept and support a grade of "Needs Improvement"—especially when I attach a comment as to why I graded that way—with much less resistance than a grade of "C," "D," or "F."

COOPERATIVE LEARNING RESEARCH

Before I learned about cooperative learning, if I wanted students to accomplish a task in groups in my Orff Schulwerk music classroom, I would quickly and haphazardly put the groups together. As you might expect, my outcomes were mediocre at best. After I studied cooperative learning, I realized that if the students didn't have the proper social skills, their outcomes always would be poor. Students need to acquire the crucial social skills of bonding through team-building activities, learning interdependence with their teammates, and spending time together to feel comfortable with each other enough to take risks. Even after I took courses in cooperative learning, I never imagined how much effort it would take for me to develop student interdependence in order to achieve high-quality outcomes. But the time I spent was well worth the effort. In the long run, I was very pleased with the students' outcomes and happy that they could work so well together. As Johnson and Johnson say: "Ensure that learning groups are truly cooperative. Cooperative learning groups are characterized by positive interdependence, individual accountability, face-to-face promotive interaction, the appropriate use of interpersonal and small-group skills, and group processing. It is cooperative learning groups that promote higher achievement, more positive relationships among students, and greater psychological health."[3] When I began, I never intended to formally research cooperative learning, but through my observations I discovered that my cooperative learning classroom was congruent with the scholarly research that I have encountered. A person might suspect that because schools work to socialize children, schools would emphasize cooperative learning. However, this is not the case. Often lab groups and special project groups use cooperative learning techniques, but these are usually a small portion of the approaches that students encounter in their day-to-day schooling. Most of the time students work independently in competition with one another. In fact, cooperative learning strategies are appropriate for more than just grade school music—they can be used at any grade level and with most academic subjects.

"The cooperative learning research indicates the importance of designing cooperative methods to resolve the problem of individual accountability. When he or she is held accountable for part of the unique task, this is most successful for increasing student achievement. Individual accountability and group rewards are necessary if cooperative learning is to have positive achievement effects. If the learning of every group member is not critical to group success, or if group success is not rewarded, achievement is unlikely to be increased above the level characteristic of traditional classrooms."[4]

Cooperative learning techniques create healthy student bonds. Allport's theory of contact of intergroup relations holds that, if individuals of different races are to develop supportive relationships,

---

3   D. W. Johnson and R. T. Johnson, "The role of cooperative learning in assessing and communicating student learning" *1996 ASCD Yearbook: Communicating Student Learning,* edited by T. R. Gusky (Alexandria, VA: Association for Supervision and Curriculum Development, 1996).

4   R. E. Slavin, *Cooperative Learning in Student Teams: What Research Says to the Teacher,* revised edition (Washington, DC: National Education Association, 1987).

they must engage in frequent cooperative activity on an equal footing.[5] If a teacher assigns students to work together on a common task toward a common goal where each individual can make substantial contribution to the mutually-desired goal, then students of diverse backgrounds will learn to like and respect one another. My observations support this theory.

My experiences also support the finding that emotionally troubled students are accepted in their team more readily than if they are merely a part of the whole class.[6] Slavin also noted that students with emotional disturbances acted more appropriately when they worked in cooperative groups.[7] Similarly, Hertz-Lazarowitz, Sharan, and Steinberg reported that students were more enthusiastic about music class and the assigned tasks when the teacher employed cooperative learning strategies.[8]

Consider cooperation and competition. Both concepts constitute relationships between two or more people; both situations are conditions of interdependence. Deutsch concluded that in either case people's "fates" are intertwined.[9] In competition, one pupil's aim or goal is in opposition to that of all the others, in that the pupil who obtains the highest grade automatically determines to some degree the fate of each of the others, and similarly the best pupil's

---

5 G. W. Allport, *The Nature of Prejudice* (Cambridge, MA: Perseus Books, 1954).

6 R. E. Slavin and A. M. Tanner, "Effects of cooperative reward structures and individual accountability on productivity and learning," *Journal of Educational Research* 72 (1979), 294–298; and S. Ziegler, "The effectiveness of cooperative learning teams for increasing cross-ethnic friendship: Additional evidence," *Human Organization* 40 (1981), 264–268.

7 R. E. Slavin, "Using student learning teams to integrate the desegregated classroom," *Integrated Education* 15 (1977), 56–58.

8 R. Hertz-Lazarowitz, S. Sharan, and R. Steinberg, "Classroom learning style and cooperative behavior of elementary school children," *Journal of Educational Psychology* 72/1 (1980), 99–106.

9 M. Deutsch, "A theory of cooperation and competition" *Human Relations* 2 (1949), 129–152.

fate depends on the other pupils doing worse. Cooperative situations have quite a different kind of interdependence. For instance, groups of students receive a grade based on the whole group's performance, and each individual's success directly depends on the success of his or her peers.

I like the idea of simultaneity in cooperative learning, and I believe that students like it, too. When students know that they will contribute equally each and every day in music class, and that their creativity will be valued by their teammates, they will be stimulated to bring excitement and anticipation to each lesson. In a traditional classroom, a teacher asks a question and one person at a time answers while the rest of the class sits and listens. In cooperative groups, a teacher asks a question and all the class answers simultaneously—each member of a team answers in their team while their teammates listen. So if your classroom has five teams, then five people (one in each team) speak to their teammates at the same time, simultaneously. Every team member gets to contribute. That's the magic of cooperative learning.

My school has a special program for students with severe emotional disturbances (SED) from kindergarten through sixth grade. In my experience, when these students are mainstreamed into a typical class, their behavior becomes less troublesome, but when they are grouped homogeneously their negative behaviors feed on one another. In a typical classroom, an SED student usually wants to fit in. And when that classroom uses cooperative learning techniques, the SED student becomes more aware of how to fit into the team. In teams, an SED student seems to experience more positive peer pressure to fit in, and beneficial results are more quickly attained. Of course, SED students can observe role models for proper behavior in classrooms that don't use cooperative learning environments, but in cooperative teams the students teach each other proper social etiquette as they work on activities together. And the positive peer pressure that the SED students feel as they acclimate to proper social etiquette reinforces the success of all the teammates. During a cooperative learning task, the teacher presents both a cooperative learning skill and a musical skill, so an SED student will shape his or her behavior to accommodate a social skill in order to get a musical task done.

Although not every SED student achieves positive results, most SED students seem to benefit. In my experience teaching SED students, I found that behavioral problems dissipated over time when the students worked within cooperative learning teams. Initially, typical students had some difficulties tolerating students with special needs, but eventually the typical students became adept at ignoring minor problems and helped to nurture the SED students to develop more acceptable team behavior. In this way, all of the students benefited from the experience: The SED students gained more peer acceptance, sometimes made friends outside their separate classroom, and acquired more confidence. And the typical students experienced a sense of leadership. But before I brought in SED students, I spoke privately with the other students in the team to explain their responsibilities for the student with special needs. I gave the team members the initiative to take the lead to help their teammate with special needs. And in the end, everyone involved felt good.

Most cooperative learning research underscores that students achieve improved self-esteem, better peer relationships, heightened enthusiasm for the subject, and improved overall achievement. Robert Marzano states, "Student achievement percentile gain when using cooperative learning is 27%."[10] R. J. Marzano, D.J. Pickering, and J.E. Pollock state, "Research shows that organizing students

---

10 Robert Marzano, *What Works in Schools: Translating Research into Action* (Alexandria VA: ASCD, 2003), 80.

into cooperative groups yields a positive effect on overall learning."[11] Patricia Shehan Campbell and Carol Scott Kassner state, in *Music in Childhood*: "Forming Cooperative Learning groups can be easy or difficult depending on the makeup of classes; their experience with Cooperative Learning, and the number of individuals who bring with them difficulties relating to others of low interpersonal intelligence. This is true to a point. However, David W. Johnson, Roger T. Johnson, E. J. Holubec, and P. Roy developed Cooperative Learning as a system to improve student learning of subject matter and help students become more interdependent, better self-managers, and more effective problem solvers. Active music-making lends itself to cooperative learning. As facilitators of these music makers, music teachers' goals are to strive for autonomy of their students, to experience positive interdependence on one another, to attain individual accountability, task completion, and improved social skills as they pertain to music making. All of the National Music Standards can be taught through cooperative learning groups."[12] Theories of learning point to the fact that an important feature of child development is enculturation, wherein children develop cognitive skills through their social and environmental backgrounds or schema. According to Jerome Bruner, students learn through exploration and problem solving, and when students participate in cooperative learning teams, they have an opportunity for social development that expands their exploration and problem solving. According to Lev Vygotsky, "Social interaction plays a fundamental role in the development of cognition. Every function in the child's cultural development appears twice: first, on

---

11 R. J. Marzano, D.J. Pickering, and J.E. Pollock, *Classroom Instruction That Works* (Alexandria, VA: ASCD, 2001).

12 Patricia Shehan Campbell and Carol Scott Kassner, *Music in Childhood*, third edition (Schirmer, 2005).

the social level, and later on the individual level; first, between people (interpsychological) and then inside the child (intrapsychological)."[13]

Students make what they learn meaningful, says David Jonassen, through constructivism. Through experiences, encounters, and interaction, the students' learning lasts longer and is more relevant. "Ownership of a problem is the key to meaningful learning."[14] In cooperative learning teams, the teacher provides students with interesting, relevant, and engaging problems to solve together. Students interact with each other to discover the solution to a given problem or task. They are co-creators of a given result and feel ownership, which leads them to a more meaningful sense of the world.

Jackie Wiggins summarizes social constructivist theory: "Children learn to become members of our society by learning from more knowledgeable members of society. We learn first by interacting with others in a social context and then by internalizing what we learn from others to the point that we are eventually able to function on our own. Children need opportunities to engage in problem solving with others."[15] She says that the implication for teachers is to include opportunities for students to interact with and receive support from more knowledgeable people around them, both teachers and peers. "The more experience the participants have working together, the higher the level of mutual understanding among community members."

However, group learning is not necessarily cooperative learning. As I demonstrated in the first few chapters of this book, cooperative learning takes a lot of preparation for both the teacher and the

---

13 L. S. Vygotsky, *Mind and Society: The Development of Higher Mental Processes* (Cambridge, MA: Harvard University Press, 1978).

14 D. H. Jonassen, "Objectism vs. constructivism: Do we need a new philosophical paradigm shift?" *Educational Technology: Research & Development* 39/3 (1991).

15 Jackie Wiggins, *Teaching for Musical Understanding* (McGraw Hill, 2001).

students. But once your preparation is in place, you can proceed with cooperative learning strategies that will enable your students to think independently and solve problems creatively as they make music.

CHAPTER ELEVEN

LESSON SUGGESTIONS

In this chapter, I present lessons using cooperative learning strategies that I have taught with great success in my music classrooms. But of course, my suggestions are merely a few of many possible ways to approach these strategies. You should always adapt my suggestions to your specific teaching situation. My lessons are only suggestions, and not intended to be followed exactly because, in the tradition of Orff Schulwerk, teaching music is comprised of speaking, singing, playing instruments, and moving. There is a myriad of ways to approach each musical concept from any angle of the components of speech, singing, instruments, or movement that will reinforce a student's understanding of a musical concept. Orff Schulwerk is not a method, but an approach that lends itself to a teacher's strengths. It also gives the students many ways to learn—tactile, kinesthetic, aural, and visual—with no particular learning mode stressed more than any other. Because Orff Schulwerk embraces exploration, improvisation, organization, and literacy, the lessons I present in this chapter can be adapted to other active music-making approaches or methods. The Dalcroze, Kodály, and Gordon approaches each include forms of these teaching techniques, but in different ways that use their own media and processes. You can adapt cooperative learning skills easily to any approach to active music-making because of the social aspect of making music together. So, just because my suggested lessons are Orff-centered, does not mean that you cannot adapt them for Kodály, Gordon, or Dalcroze-centered lessons. Cooperative learning objectives apply to all active-music-making approaches.

If your students have little expertise with active music making, then you might need to pare down the process to fit your students' abilities. Remember that every student moves at a different pace, so you might have better success if you divide a complicated lesson into many simpler sections. These lessons are not targeted to any particular grade level, because musical skill and training vary so widely from school to school. If your students are very accomplished in speaking, playing instruments, creating movements, singing (with solfeggio, numbers, or letters), any method of composing, improvising, exploring, and ultimately reading music, then you can use these suggested lessons with younger and younger students. But if your students have not had many opportunities to develop their musical skills or use these teaching techniques, then you ought to raise the grade level and modify the suggestions in the lessons to suit the age level and experience of your students, and your time limitations. At first, you won't have success with every lesson. Not all lessons will match your teaching style. Teaching is an art—you are the facilitator of music-making in your classroom. And, as always, when you prepare any music lesson using cooperative learning strategies, make sure you have both a musical objective and a cooperative objective. Best wishes for much success!

I. THINK—PAIR—SHARE ACTIVITY

Music Objective: Experience staccato and legato articulations

Cooperative Learning Objective: Share ideas

Process:

1. The teacher reads two poems that demonstrate staccato and legato articulations: "Nonsense" (from *Crackers and Crumbs* by Sonja Dunn) and "Popalong Hopcorn!" (from *Tasty Poems* collected by Jill Bennett).

2. The students echo each poem.

3. Each student thinks about how he or she would move his or her arms to each of the poems.

4. Students partner up and share their ideas. Together, pairs of students think how to move different parts of their bodies, and then partners share their ideas.

5. One of the partners gets a white board, a dry marker, and an eraser. Partners think how they would draw a picture of the way their arms moved. Partners share their ideas.

6. Together, partners create a dance for each poem. Also, partners choose instruments to accompany their dance for each poem.

7. Partners share their ideas with the whole class. Evaluate the effectiveness of the instruments the students chose to illustrate staccato and legato.

    (*This activity is based on a strategy by Mary Palmer.*)

II. Inside—Outside Circle Activity

Music Objective: More experience with staccato and legato articulations

Cooperative Learning Objective: Take turns

Process:

1. Before the activity begins, the teacher obtains postcard-size prints of famous pieces of art that students will use to represent staccato and legato articulations. Put these prints into a box or a hat for students to draw out of.

2. The students pair up and arrange themselves into two concentric circles, the pairs of students facing each other. The student in the inside circle draws a print from the box. The pairs take turns creating sounds to represent the form of the print they selected from the box. After a few minutes of experimentation, the pairs decide what sounds fit best with their print. Each pair selects a spokesperson who describes and demonstrates to the whole class what the pair discovered about the sounds that their print evoked.

3. The students stand, and as the teacher plays music, one circle of students moves counter-clockwise while the other stays still. When the music stops, the circle stops moving and the students pair up again with new partners. Then the pairs select new prints from the box, and the activity repeats. Repeat the activity several times.

4. Still using inside and outside circles, the teacher plays a recording of part of Scarlatti's Concerto grosso No. 5 in D minor (Allegro). Each pair decides whether the musical articulations are staccato or legato and shows their choice by moving their bodies while standing in the same spot. The pairs share with the whole class, and everyone evaluates whether the motions fit with the music. Repeat this activity with Beethoven's Piano Sonata No. 14 in C-sharp minor, Op. 27 No. 2 "Moonlight."

III. Think—Pair—Squared—Share Activity

Music Objective: Experience contemporary music

Cooperative Learning Objective: Use time wisely

Process:

1. The teacher shows the students a series of vocabulary words showing on-the-spot, non-locomotive movements— which are movements students can do while they stand in one place—such as bend, twist, jump, twirl, stretch, flick, dab, freeze, etc. For each vocabulary word in the list, the teacher first models the movement, and then the students perform the movement.

2. Each student thinks of four contrasting words from the vocabulary list and puts them in a sequence they like. Students can repeat words, if they want to. Each student's sequence will be different and last a different length of time. At the end of his or her sequence, the student freezes in a statue, the pose resulting from the last on-the-spot movement.

3. Students each practice the motions in their sequence by themselves until they feel comfortable and really like what they created.

4. Students pair up and share each other's sequences. The pairs move in their sequences at the same time and then

collaborate to make their motions contrast, particularly at the beginning and the ending, when they freeze in their statues. If one of the pair's on-the-spot movements seems too similar, partners should change their sequence to create an interesting contrast. The sequences shouldn't be the same, but each partner should perform his or her own sequence being aware of the other. It is fine if one person's sequence ends before the other's sequence. Then, the whole class performs at once with all pairs moving in their sequences at the same time.

5. Each pair combines with another pair to form a team of four. The team pools its sequences so that the movements contrast and the beginnings and endings are interesting, contrasting, and connecting. At the end of the team's sequence, everyone should freeze in a statue with a contrasting pose. Then, each team performs their sequences all at once in front of the whole class. Once again, it is fine if some students finish their sequences earlier than others in the team.

6. The teacher plays a recording of part of Stockhausen's *Klavierstücke V* to accompany the whole class performing their team sequences at once. Afterwards, let the students talk within their teams to discuss how the music made their dances feel differently. Then, have all the teams share their discoveries with the whole class. Evaluate the results of each team and how each team's sequence differed from one another. Talk about individual variations as a class.

IV. Groups of Four—Roundtable Activity

Music Objective: Review of non-pitched percussion families

Cooperative Learning Objective: Work together without talking

Process:

1. Get into teams, and have each team's materials person get a piece of paper and a pencil. Explain that during the activity the students pass the pencil and paper around the team so that each team member can write one answer and then pass the pencil and paper to the next student. The team will make a list for each team to review and discuss later.

2. Explain that the students will keep passing the pencil and paper around the team until time is up. Encourage the students to pass the paper and pencil quickly, and if a student cannot think of something to write, then pass the paper and pencil onto the next teammate. Time is of the essence.

3. Tell the students to write a list of non-pitched wood percussion instruments in one column on the piece of paper, non-pitched metals in another, and non-pitched skins in a third. Remind the students that they should not talk or else their team will be disqualified. It's okay not to get the spelling exactly right. Then say: "Ready, set, go!"

4. When the teacher announces time is up, all the students put their hands on their heads, and the last person writing drops the pencil and paper on the floor. Then the materials person returns the pencil.

5. Each team shares its list with the class. The team with the most instruments correct wins a reward.

V. Three-Step Interview Activity

Music Objective: Learn the names of pitched and non-pitched instruments

Cooperative Learning Objective: Ask effective questions and play instruments quietly

Process:

1. Create necklaces out of yarn with a small sentence strip attached on which is written the name of each Orff instrument. The instrument names will hang on the back of each student, so that others can see, but the student who is wearing the necklace with the name cannot.

2. The object of the activity is for each student to identify the instrument written on the back of his or her necklace by playing a game of questions and answers with another student. Partner up.

3. The teacher models the question and answer interview process: "Am I a pitched instrument? (Yes.) Am I the largest pitched instrument? (No.) Am I the smallest pitched instrument? (No.) Do I have metal bars? (Yes.) Am I an Alto Metallophone? (Yes!)"

4. Instruct the students to ask their partners questions that can be answered with only "yes" or "no." The question and answer interview continues until the student gets the right answer. If some students get stuck, the teacher or partner may give hints. After one student guesses his or her instrument correctly, the students exchange roles.

5. After both students know their instruments, they help each other to find their instrument and bring it back to their spots. But they shouldn't play it yet.

6. When everyone has their instruments, the teacher reviews the names of each of the instruments and shows how to play them correctly using the proper technique.

7. Pairs of students combine to form teams of four to share the name of their instruments, and explain how they are played. Then, let the teams exchange instruments with other teams and explore their sounds quietly.

(This activity is based on a strategy by Susan Krissoff.)

VI. Circle of Knowledge Activity

Music Objective: Recognize notation

Cooperative Learning Objective: Invites others to contribute

Process:

1. Each team selects a category (sports, colors, food, fruits, etc.) and creates a list of words in that category that can fit various rhythms that the class has been working on recently (quarter notes, eighth notes, sixteenth notes, dotted eighth-sixteenth notes, syncopations, and so on). The words they choose must fit naturally with the rhythm of the notes. As team members suggest words, one person in the team (the "recorder") writes the words under the notated rhythm with the help of the rest of the team.

2. Using their lists of words, each team creates a rhythmic phrase at least eight beats long from the word patterns they have chosen. (See example.) Next, the team makes a poster of their rhythmic phrase, but showing the rhythm only, not the words. The team decides on a family of non-pitched instruments to perform the rhythm, and practices speaking the words as they play the rhythm on their instruments. After the team is secure doing this, then they should silently think the words and only play the rhythm of the words on their instruments.

   Words and Rhythms:

   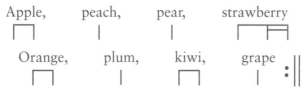

3. When the teams are ready, they mount their posters on the wall so that the whole class can see them. Then, each team performs its rhythmic piece, first with words, then with only instruments. All the other teams should look at the rhythms on the posters and decide which one the team is playing.

4. The class should discuss the ways they supported each other while they participated in this activity.

(This activity is based on a strategy by Phyllis Kaplan and Sandra Stauffer.)

VII. SEND A PROBLEM ACTIVITY

Music Objective: Identify and use techniques to vary a melody

Cooperative Learning Objective: Stay on task

Process:

1. Review various ways a person can change a melody. Write down these ways in a "How to vary a melody" list on the board.

2. Have the students team up, and then get some barred instruments, two instruments per team of four.

3. Teach the students "Twinkle, Twinkle, Little Star" via solfegge. First, introduce the key you will play in by singing: "C is Do today, D is Re, E is Mi today, F is Fa, G is Sol, A is La." Sing and play "Twinkle, Twinkle, Little Star," and let the students echo you. Those team members without instruments should sing and use the Curwen hand signs. After a couple of times through, have teammates exchange roles by switching those who play the instruments and those who sing. Make sure everyone can perform the melody.

4. Have the teams check each team member's ability to play the melody. The team makes sure each team member can play the melody correctly. Then, referring back to the "How to vary a melody" list, each team member should suggest a possible variation for the melody. The team should choose one or more of the methods of variation and prepare their own variation of "Twinkle, Twinkle, Little Star." The team lists the ways that they have varied the melody on a piece of paper to give to the teacher.

5. After rehearsing, each team should perform its variation by having all four teammates play simultaneously on their instruments while the rest of the class listens for what ways the performers varied the melody. The rest of the class should try to determine the ways how the performing team made its variation. When the class reaches its solution, the teacher tells the class how the team varied the melody. The teams switch roles so that each team has an opportunity to perform its variation.

6. Determine an order for each team's variation, and perform (and record) a "Theme and Variations." Play back the recording, and let the class evaluate and discuss what they liked about each variation, and what they might do differently the next time they vary a tune to make it better.

7. Listen to a portion of Mozart's Variations K265 and K455 performed by Andras Schiff. (Perhaps listen only to the theme and the first few variations, not the whole piece.) Discuss the ways Mozart used to vary his theme.

(This activity is based on a strategy by Lisa DeLorenzo.)

VIII. NUMBERED HEADS TOGETHER ACTIVITY

Music Objective: Create movement for a canon

Cooperative Learning Objective: Speak quietly while working in teams

Process:

1. Teach the canon "Mi Gallo" by singing, then having the students echo you, phrase by phrase.

2. Model various possibilities for movement, and have the students mirror you.

3. Remind the students of their numbers within their teams. When the teacher calls out a number, that person becomes the team leader. The leader makes movements and the rest of the team members mirror the leader's motions. After a short while, the teacher calls out another number, and that team member becomes leader. Each person should get an opportunity to be leader several times. After this, the teacher asks the students to recall the movements that they liked best during the activity and the movements that provided the most contrast. (The teacher should demonstrate movements that seem too similar and those that seem very contrasting.)

4. Each team uses the ideas from the mirroring to create movement to accompany the canon "Mi Gallo."

5. After rehearsing, each team shares its movements for the canon with the whole class.

6. Discuss which team's movement canons were most effective and why. The teacher could call out numbers, and students with that number could stand and share their thoughts.

MI GALLO SE MURIÓ

Traditional French canon, translated in Spanish

Mi ga - llo se mu - rió a - yer,

Mi ga - llo se mu - rió a - yer,

Ya no can - ta - rá co - co - di, co - co - da,

Ya no can - ta - rá co - co - di, co - co - da,

Co - co - di co - di co - co - di, co - co - da.

IX. Jigsaw Activity

Music Objective: Build musical listening skills

Cooperative Learning Objective: Learn to listen to each other

Process:

1. Out of the original teams, all students of the same number form new groups (all the "ones" meet together, all the "twos," etc.). Give each new group one piece of a puzzle on which is a listening question (as shown below). Members of each group should work together to answer the listening question posed by their puzzle piece. Appoint one student in each group to monitor the group's ability to speak using quiet voices and to talk one at a time. Take turns speaking, using chips: each person in the group gets the same number of chips, and each time a person wishes to speak, he or she places one chip in the center of the group. When a person's chips are gone, he or she is finished talking.

    Puzzle Pieces:

    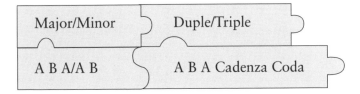

2. Listen several times to the "Berceuse" from the Keetman Collection *Musik für Kinder-Orff Schulwerk* and discuss what you hear each time. Then, the new group members should return to their original teams to "put the puzzle together." That is, the team members share what they

discovered in their new groups and learn from their teammates. Then, play the "Berceuse" again so that the students have one last chance to listen for the musical elements that their team members described.

3. Finally, let the teams each create a dance that reflects the form, meter, and style of the "Berceuse."

4. After rehearsal, the teams should share their dances with the whole class and discuss how their dance reflects what they hear in the music.

(This activity is based on a strategy by Phyllis Kaplan and Sandra Stauffer.)

X. Game Activity

Music Objective: Learn the classroom rules

Cooperative Learning Objective: Build team spirit–work together

Process:

1. Beforehand, make puzzles for each team. On the puzzle pieces, write the five classroom rules ("Raise your hand to speak," "Put materials back where they belong," etc.), one word for each puzzle piece. Then, put the puzzle pieces in sealed envelopes, one envelope for each member of each team, and number each set of envelopes one through five.

2. Give each team a set of envelopes. Each team member takes the envelope labeled with his or her number within the team. Don't open the envelopes yet: their contents are a mystery.

3. At your signal, all the team members empty the contents of their envelopes and turn over all the puzzle pieces so that the whole team can see the words. Tell the teams to put the puzzles together to make five complete sentences, but without talking. Any talking disqualifies the team. The first team to put together the puzzles properly, wins!

XI. ANOTHER GAME ACTIVITY

Music Objective: Music repertoire review

Cooperative Learning Objective: Building team spirit by working together

Process:

1. Assemble in teams of four. One student (the "recorder") writes down as many songs as the team can think of that have color words in the lyrics (yellow, brown, red, etc.) For example, "Yellow Bird" is a good choice, but *Greensleeves* is not because it does not have "green" in the lyrics, only the title. The team should brainstorm as many songs as possible within your pre-determined time limit.

2. The teacher spins to determine which team should begin, and calls out a color such as "brown." The team going first sings part of a song with that color on their list. (Like "John Brown's Body.") Each team gets one point for each song they sing. Then, the teacher spins to choose another team. No team is allowed to repeat a song that another team already has sung. The team with the most points at the end wins.

Conclusion

You, as teacher, should feel free to adapt any of these lessons to your particular situation. Remember to use the musical and cooperative concepts that you are working on at the time. Consider the National Standards for Music Education and how your cooperative learning strategies will help your students achieve all of the standards. If any lesson does not work to your satisfaction on the first try, don't give up. Keep practicing—both you and your students will improve. Try a lesson a different way, focused on a different cooperative learning skill. If everything you did was perfect on the first try, you wouldn't get the satisfaction of learning. Great teachers are always learning— just like their students.

Action Plans

Chapter One Action Plan

- Be well-organized
- Take time to prepare students
- Communicate with parents and students

Chapter Two Action Plan

- Share goals with the students
- Role-play, find ways to demonstrate similarities and differences
- Find ways to practice conflict resolution
- Role-play ways to show kindness
- Demonstrate body language
- Prepare students for working in groups—voice volumes, not interrupting

- Prepare students to ask questions
- Explain and practice time management
- Consider assigning team roles

Chapter Three Action Plan

- Organize your bookkeeping
- Create class lists for each classroom including team letter and number
- Decide how many teams and how many students in each team
- Make team letters
- Create games for students to remember their teams and numbers
- Organize and label everything in your classroom for easy use
- Explain your expectations when students get out and put away materials
- Make spinners
- Decide how to group students

Chapter Four Action Plan

- Prepare students for good behavior
- Prepare students to share with each other
- Prepare students to be kind to each other
- Role-play how to show kindness
- Create a poster of kindness phrases
- Prepare students to listen
- Prepare students to resolve conflicts
- Prepare students to compromise
- Prepare students to work equally

- Prepare students how to get the job done—create a poster
- Model, model, model

Chapter Five Action Plan

- Develop team-building activities
- Take time to create team names
- Take time to create team handshakes
- Make time for teams to create their own identity
- Develop team rules
- Make time for team members to discover things in common

Chapter Six Action Plan

- Review process with students
- Write down steps for students
- Write down the time allotted for each step
- Facilitate time or assign a timer, depending on students' age
- Allow the students to be the teacher
- Model lessons
- Remind students of the cooperative skills that they need to complete the task

Chapter Seven Action Plan

- Prepare monthly student music evaluation sheets
- Prepare monthly student cooperative skills sheets
- Prepare monthly student behavior sheets
- Keep up with monthly bookkeeping for each class to simplify evaluation and grading

Chapter Eight Action Plan

- Become familiar with cooperative learning structures useful in active music making
- Puzzles
- Think-Pair-Share
- Think-Pair-Squared-Share
- Inside—Outside Circle
- Three-Step Interview
- Circle of Knowledge
- Send a Problem
- Numbered Heads Together
- Jigsaw
- Games Activities

Chapter Nine Action Plan

- Become familiar with cooperative learning skills for easy student assessment
- Become a careful observer
- Circulate throughout the classroom—it's imperative
- For student to student assessment, list what to listen and look for—objective standards
- Consider separate grades for growth in musical skills, cooperative skills, and behavior
- Consider grading with "Outstanding," "Satisfactory," and "Needs Improvement," rather than letter grades

Chapter Ten Action Plan

- Become familiar with cooperative learning research
- Take a cooperative learning course
- Consider keeping teams together during an entire grading period to ensure bonding
- Work for team loyalty through team-building activities
- Hold each team member accountable for resolving problems
- Reward successful teams
- Assign students a common task leading to a common goal
- Consider setting cooperative teams in competition with other cooperative teams—success is dependent on individuals working together
- Simultaneity creates anticipation for and enthusiasm in each lesson
- Mainstreaming special education students within cooperative teams improves individual and peer esteem
- End-products of cooperative learning are improved self-esteem, better relationships, heightened enthusiasm for the subject, and improved achievement

Chapter Eleven Action Plan

- When you prepare a music lesson plan, make sure you combine a musical concept with a cooperative learning skill
- Review each cooperative learning structure before choosing one to use for your lesson
- When introducing your lesson to your students, model first
- Clarify for the students both the cooperative learning skill and the musical concept
- Make sure students know the sequence of the steps in order to achieve the goal or solve the problem
- Make sure students know how much time to spend on each step
- Remind students how to get the job done (look at your poster)
- Remind students how to be mannerly (look at your poster)
- Remind students how to resolve conflicts (look at your poster)
- Remind students what you will be looking for

CODA: A GREAT ACT TO FOLLOW

By JENNA KIRK

I was blessed to have one of the greatest first jobs a new music teacher could have—not only did I get to take over an active music-making classroom, but I also returned to the same classroom where I completed my student teaching with Carol Huffman before she retired. Imagine! Starting my first day of teaching already familiar with the staff, principal, students, and classroom routines. This was the situation in which I was fortunate enough to find myself, and it has been a dream! With Carol's cooperative learning methods already in place, I just took the principles I had experienced in my student teaching and put my own spin on them. And after I read this book, one of Carol's ideas that I like most is that a teacher can use whatever parts of any cooperative learning concepts he or she feels appropriate for his or her classroom.

When I began my job, I immediately realized that my students were genuinely excited to create music. And even though I was just beginning my teaching career, I already had a sense of the advanced skills that these students exhibited in terms of their communication, decision-making, confidence, and creativity. During my first year of teaching, I also taught two extra music classes at another school that did not have previous experience with cooperative learning. For most of the school year, I struggled to teach these students how to make decisions quickly and harmoniously, to perform with confidence, and to reach the highest levels of thinking. But by the last quarter of the school year, my music classes were a fairly smoothly-running machine buzzing efficiently with rules, routines, and arrangements. After going through these struggles and finding success through my persistence with cooperative learning techniques, I am a firm believer that they definitely work!

One of my favorite experiences with cooperative learning is the first day we create teams with the youngest students. (Because I student taught during the third quarter of the school year, I never had the chance see how thrilling this was for the youngest students.) We spend a few minutes talking about how exciting it is to have teammates, that music is meant to be shared, and how all the students in the whole school use teams. Then, once the students are genuinely pumped-up enough, we assign teams. In my experience, the bigger the deal I make about the students' new teams, the better they perform.

Through my experiences student teaching with Carol, I realized the importance of positive reinforcement, a concept championed by many knowledgeable educators. I built on the cooperative learning teams that were already in place, and started using a system of "Team Points" as a method of positive reinforcement. I track the points that students earn on a dry-erase board on the front wall. Each time a team does something noteworthy (for example, be the first team ready for activities, have teammates work together nicely, participate exceptionally, perform outstandingly, etc.), a team member gets to add a point for their team on the dry-erase board. At the end of class, the team with the most points wins a reward. After trying lots of different rewards, I decided the best one was to have the students "autograph" their name on a "Musicians of the Week" dry-erase board. (This reward is something they can be proud of, and it is *free* to maintain after the initial purchase—no more buying prizes or candy!) This reward system has lots of benefits. First of all, students love to walk up to the board and add a point in front of everyone else. Meanwhile, if one team demonstrates some negative behavior (like being "chatty"), I often award points to all the other teams that listen attentively. The "chatty" team will definitely get the hint, and I don't have to follow through with any consequences. Also, this rewards system enables students to use higher-level thinking skills. I often ask the teams to evaluate performances and vote on their favorite; the teams that receive the most votes are awarded extra points.

Overall, using Carol's methods to integrate cooperative learning into my classroom has made my experiences as a music teacher much more rewarding. One of my favorite aspects of using cooperative teams occurs during those infrequent times in class when I lecture or explain about music. Instead of asking a rhetorical or simple-answer question and calling on only one student to answer, I enjoy asking a question to the class as a whole. Then I say, "Talk to your team and see what they think." After I give them a chance to discuss the question, I'll ask a team to share its ideas, but I'll only call on a team with everyone raising their hands in agreement, because that means they have already come up with a consensus (higher-level thinking skills, again!). This is my favorite way to facilitate class discussions— even those students who are the most challenging to motivate get involved.

I realize I still have a lot to experience and to learn as a music teacher, but I am already convinced of the positive effects of cooperative learning. Every once in a while, a student (often new to our school and our music room routines) does not feel comfortable in this kind of social environment. To address this discomfort, the whole class discusses how music is so often a *social* art, and how important it is to experience music with other people (even after experiencing it for yourself). I feel that—for so many reasons—any teacher's active music-making classroom will benefit from incorporating even a minimal amount of Carol's cooperative learning techniques.

WILDFLOWER COVER

I chose wildflowers for the book cover because Carl Orff said that teaching with his Orff Schulwerk was like sowing seeds to create wildflowers, and that the wildflowers spread with sunshine and water, much like a teacher's care in the classroom nurtures children as they learn how to make music.

I quote Professor Doctor Carl Orff's speech at the inauguration of the Orff Institute in Salzburg on October 25, 1961 (published by B. Schotts, Mainz in the *Orff Institute Jahrbuch* 1963, translated by Margaret Murray):

"Looking back, I should like to describe Schulwerk as a wild flower. I am a passionate gardener so this description seems to me a very suitable one. As in Nature plants establish themselves where they are needed and where conditions are favorable, so Schulwerk has grown from ideas that were rife at the time and that found their favorable conditions in my work. Schulwerk did not develop from any preconsidered plan; I could never have imagined such a far-reaching one; but it came from a need that I was able to recognize as such. It is an experience of long standing that wild flowers always prosper, where carefully planned, cultivated plants often produce disappointing results.

Every phase of Schulwerk will always produce stimulation for new independent growth; therefore it is never conclusive and settled, but always developing, always growing, always flowing."

INDEX

ABOUT THE AUTHOR

Carol Huffman has taught and lectured about music education throughout the United States, Canada, and as far afield as Dalian, China. Her passion is to teach children to connect music- reading fluency with performance skills through the Orff Schulwerk approach. Throughout her many years as teacher, she has devoted herself to incorporate cooperative learning strategies into her music lessons, and the tremendous enthusiasm of her students in music class spurred by their constant opportunities to contribute has made an enormously positive difference in her teaching. She holds a Bachelor of Music Education degree from Indiana University and a Master of Arts in Education with a reading emphasis from Baldwin Wallace College. She recently retired after thirty years of teaching kindergarten through sixth grade at the Parma City School District outside of Cleveland, Ohio, where she supervised student teachers from Baldwin Wallace College. She received the Martha Holden Jennings Scholar award for outstanding teaching, and she holds a commendation from her school district's superintendent for excellence in the classroom. In the summers, she taught for eighteen years in the Orff Schulwerk Teacher Education Program at Hofstra University in Hempstead, New York. She has served on the American Orff-Schulwerk Board of Trustees and is past president of American Orff-Schulwerk Association. Since 2004, she has been included in Who's Who of American Women, and she is a contributing writer for the McGraw-Hill music series Spotlight on Music. She has been a consultant for the Kennedy Center for the Performing Arts in Washington, D.C. and served as the Executive Director of the Bloomington (Indiana) Early Music Festival, a non-profit organization dedicated to bringing Medieval, Renaissance, Baroque, and early Classical music to audiences through educational and performance events.

She is currently an Adjunct Professor at Indiana University's Jacob School of Music, where she teaches courses in Early Childhood Music and Methods, and Materials for Teaching Elementary General Music. She lives in Bloomington, Indiana with her husband of forty-one years, Phil; and she loves reading, gourmet cooking, throwing pots, and playing the piano every day.